Embellish
Your T-Shirt

Embellish Your T-Shirt

50 WAYS TO CREATE YOUR OWN STYLE, INCLUDES
35 STEP-BY-STEP PROJECTS

Katie Cole

CICO BOOKS

LONDON NEW YORK

Published in 2007 by CICO Books
an imprint of Ryland Peters & Small
20–21 Jockey's Fields, London WC1R 4BW

10 9 8 7 6 5 4 3 2 1

Text © Katie Cole 2007
Design and photography © CICO Books 2007

A CIP catalogue record for this book is available from the British Library

ISBN-13: 978 1 904991 58 8
ISBN-10: 1 904991 58 0

Printed in China

Editor: Sarah Hoggett
Designer: Ian Midson
Styled photography: Tino Tedaldi, except pages 5, 6, 8 (top left), 10,
13 (top right), 31, 40 (top right), 43, 45 (top right), 58, 73, 75 (top right),
90 (top right), 93 and 95 (top right) which are by Lucinda Symons
Step-by-step photography: Antoine Soto
Template artworks: Stephen Dew

Contents

Introduction

T-shirts must be among the most versatile of all garments and look great with both casual jeans for everyday wear and flowing skirts or tailored trousers for a special occasion. But let's be honest: solid-coloured, mass-produced T-shirts can be rather boring! *Embellish Your T-shirt* is packed with ideas that will allow you to create highly individual, personalized designs in next to no time.

From really cool street clothes, such as the little boy's zipped T-shirt on page 20, to eye-catching party outfits that are every little princess's dream (page 26), find out how you can transform your kids' T-shirts into trendy tops that will be the envy of all their friends. Chill out in embroidered and hand-painted tops inspired by Indian or North African textiles (pages 42 and 64). And for special occasions, get ready to strut your stuff in beaded, lace-trimmed, sequinned creations worthy of any Milan or Paris fashion house!

Even old T-shirts that are well past their best can be cut up and pressed into service. By recycling, you'll not only be doing your bit towards the environment, but you'll also be saving yourself a fortune – and creating unique, one-off pieces of clothing into the bargain.

The real joy of all this is that all the projects in this book can be created with minimal sewing skills in very little time. *Embellish Your T-shirt* is packed with ideas which you can either copy exactly or adapt to suit your own tastes and materials. So pick up a needle and thread, ransack your local craft store for some fun and funky embellishments and set to work!

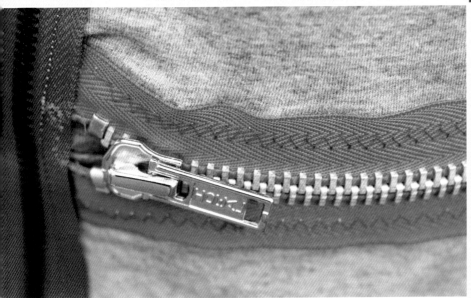

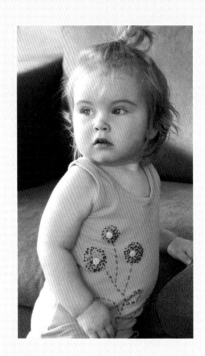

COOL KIDS

All of a flutter

Kids love brightly-coloured motifs and this hand-painted butterfly is guaranteed to have your little ones fluttering with delight! It's also a really quick-and-easy way of jazzing up a plain T-shirt for the summer. Choose a T-shirt in a pale, neutral colour so that the motif really stands out.

YOU WILL NEED
- T-shirt
- Template on page 125
- Baking or tracing paper
- Black pen
- Iron-on transfer pencil
- Iron
- Fabric paint in your chosen colour
- Paintbrush
- Iron-on printed fabric tape

1 Copy the motif on page 125 at 100 per cent and use a fine black pen to trace it onto baking or tracing paper.

2 Turn the paper over and go over the lines again, using an iron-on transfer pencil.

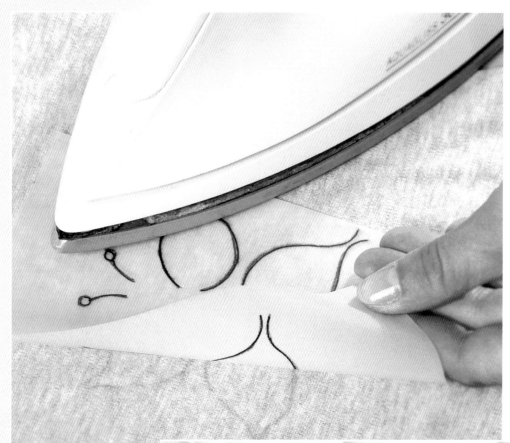

3 Place the tracing paper pencil side down on the T-shirt, centring the motif. Iron, following the pencil manufacturer's instructions, to transfer the motif to the fabric.

TIP

An iron-on transfer pencil is the easiest way to transfer motifs that you are going to paint or embroider onto fabric. Remember, however, that it makes a permanent mark that will not rub or wash out. If you're worried about the transferred lines being visible in the finished garment, use a non-permanent marker. With some brands you can simply rub out the marks with your fingers or spray them with water – and there are even brands that fade completely after a couple of days. Ask your local craft or haber-dashery store for more information.

4 Dilute the fabric paint. Place a sheet of plastic or a magazine inside the T-shirt to prevent the paint from seeping through to the back, and paint the motif. Leave to dry.

BOLD AND BRIGHT!

The vibrant pink colour of the painted motif is echoed in the printed cotton tape. If you can't find a suitable tape, or don't want to go to the expense of getting one specially made, cut a small piece of non-frayable fabric, such as felt, for the butterfly's body and stick it in place with fabric adhesive.

5 Cut a piece of printed iron-on fabric tape the length of the butterfly's body. Following the manufacturer's instructions, iron it in place.

Two of a kind

For a splash of summer sunshine, embroider matching T-shirts for Mum and baby with tiny daisylike flowers. Only two stitches – straight stitches and French knots – are used in this design, and the flower 'centres' are nothing more than a pretty pearl button, so the T-shirts are really quick and easy to decorate. Of course, if you're keen on embroidery, you could devise your own stitch plan. This kind of trailing motif looks best applied to one side of the T-shirt, rather than centred.

YOU WILL NEED

- T-shirts
- Templates on page 122
- Baking or tracing paper
- Pencil
- Iron-on transfer pencil
- Iron
- Pearl buttons in two sizes
- Embroidery threads in your chosen colours
- Embroidery needle
- Embroidery hoop

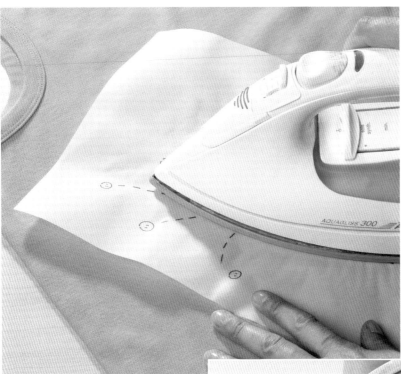

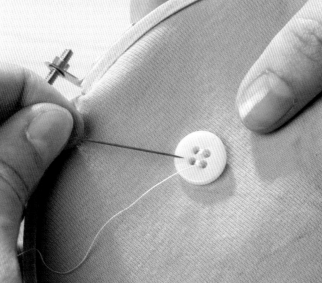

1 Trace the baby's template on page 122 at 100 per cent. Enlarge the Mum's design by 165 per cent and trace. Turn the paper over and draw over the lines with an iron-on transfer pencil. Place it pencil side down on the T-shirts and iron, following the instructions.

2 Sew on buttons (small ones for baby's T-shirt, large ones for Mum's) for the flower centres, leaving space around them for the embroidered 'petals'.

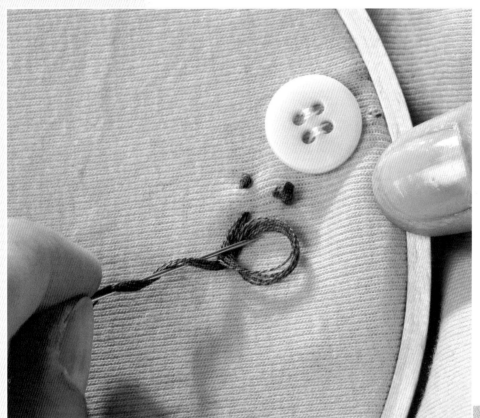

3 Place the area of the T-shirt that you want to embroider in an embroidery hoop, and work French knots around each button (see Tips, below, for technique).

TIPS

Make sure that the fabric in the embroidery hoop is neither too taut nor too loose.

To work French knots, bring the needle up at the point where the knot is required, hold the thread taut and wind it twice around the needle tip. Still holding the thread, insert the needle close to the point at which it first emerged and pull it through to the back of the work.

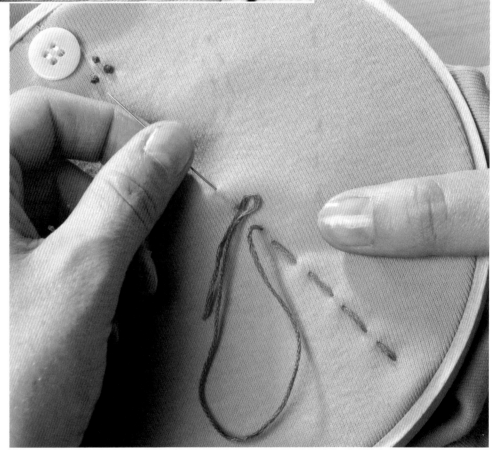

4 For the stems, work straight stitches about 4 mm/⅛ in. long along the broken lines on the embroidery template.

FLOWER POWER

The buttons and French knots give the flower heads a lovely, textural quality. Use two (or more) contrasting colours of embroidery thread for the French knots and space the knots randomly for a more natural look.

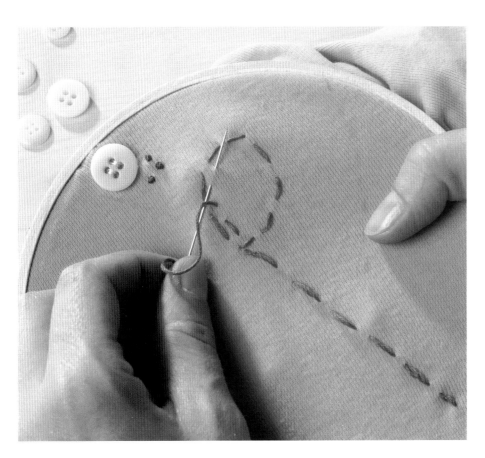

5 Embroider the leaves in the same way, working three rows of stitches for each leaf.

Ribbon wrap

A stylish ribbon and a few squares of white fabric are all you need to transform a simple white T-shirt into a trendy top. Combine with jeans or cropped trousers to make a simple but sophisticated-looking fashion statement – just what every young girl wants! A zip is set into the side seam to make it easier to pull the garment on and off; the zip needs to be 0.5 cm/¼ in. longer than the distance from the bottom of the armhole to the ribbon line.

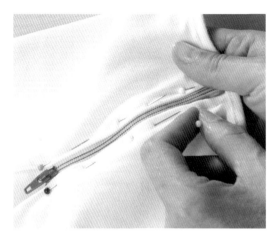

1 Unpick one side seam of the T-shirt from the point at which you want to start fixing the fabric pieces up to the base of the armhole. Pin, then machine stitch the zip in place, with the zip slider at the bottom of the unpicked section of seam.

2 Mark the ribbon line. Fold in one corner of each square and crease. Right sides together, with the folded-in corners at the base of the T-shirt, pin the squares around the T-shirt along the marked line, overlapping them slightly to form a 'skirt'.

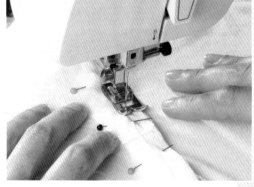

3 Using matching sewing thread, machine stitch the squares in place, stitching along the marked line.

4 Pin the decorative ribbon over the edge of the T-shirt and the fabric 'skirt' from side seam to side seam, turning under the ends to prevent the ribbon from unravelling. Stitch along the top and bottom edges of the ribbon, by hand or by machine.

5 Cut all around the base of the T-shirt, level with the end of the white zip.

19

Zipping along

Bright zips in bold, primary colours are a fun and funky way of livening up a plain, grey T-shirt. In this design they're also functional, as they hold in place a handy 'kangaroo-style' pouch or pocket for all the bits and pieces that young boys like to carry around with them!

YOU WILL NEED

- Long sleeveless grey T-shirt
- Blue zip half the width of the T-shirt
- 23-cm/9-in. green zip for back of T-shirt
- 23-cm/9-in. yellow zip for side seam
- Red zip the length of the T-shirt less 15 cm/ 6 in.
- Fabric adhesive
- Sewing threads in zip colours
- Sewing machine with zip foot
- Pinking shears

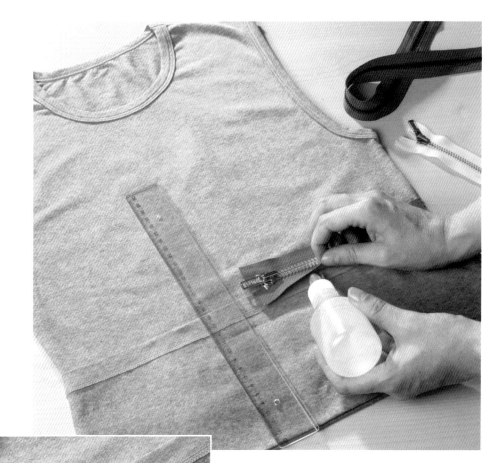

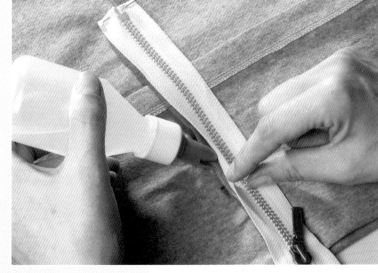

1 Fold up the bottom of the T-shirt by 15 cm/6 in. all around. Position the bottom teeth of the blue zip along the top of the turned-up section, running from the side seam to the centre front. Glue in place with fabric adhesive, then zigzag machine stitch along each side of the zip tape to secure. Attach a green zip to the centre back in the same way.

2 Position the yellow side-seam zip so that the slider end is level with the bottom of the turned-up section. Glue and then machine stitch it in place.

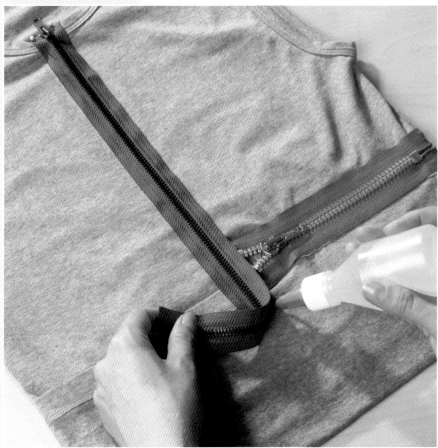

3 Position the closed red zip down the centre front of the T-shirt. Turn the open end of the zip tape over to the inside of the neck opening and then glue the whole zip, including the turned-over section of tape, in place.

TIPS

Fabric adhesive holds the zips in place securely so that you can machine stitch without the risk of breaking the needle by stitching over pins.

A zip foot attachment for your sewing machine will make this project much easier. The needle can be used on each side of the foot in turn, so that you can stitch really close to the zip teeth.

Stitch light-coloured zips in place using a contrasting colour of thread for extra impact.

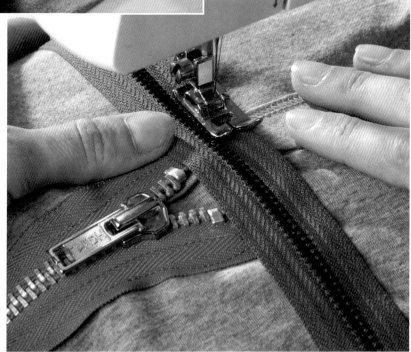

4 Machine stitch along both sides of the tape, making sure the red zip does not go over the top stop of the blue zip.

COLOUR CONTRASTS

The contrasting colours of the zips are what really make this design. Remember to think about the colour of the zip teeth, as well as the colour of the zips themselves. Here, the red zip has black teeth (a classic and dramatic colour combination), while the blue zip has shiny, metallic teeth.

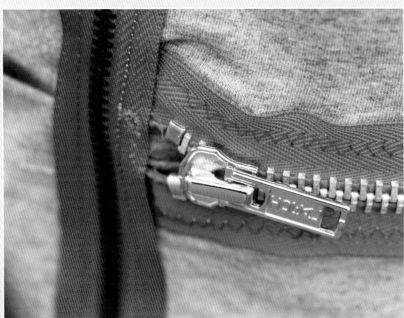

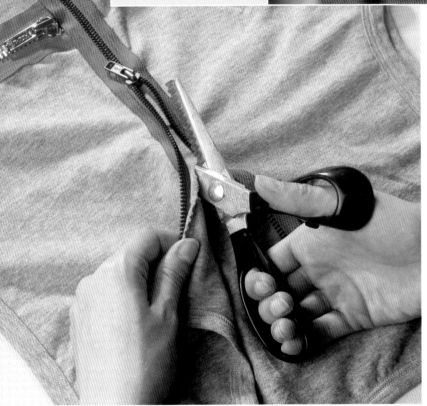

5 Open the centre zip, then cut the T-shirt fabric between the two rows of teeth, taking great care not to cut into the stitches. Trim the cut edges of the T-shirt fabric with pinking shears to reduce the risk of fraying.

Chic chick

Attaching a silk scarf, casually knotted at the side, is a really simple way of transforming a plain T-shirt into an elegant dress. Add a flowing, hand-painted motif and you've got a chic, 'designer' look that will make every young girl feel like a supermodel strutting her stuff on the catwalk!

1 Enlarge the template on page 120 by 171 per cent, and trace it onto baking or tracing paper. Turn it over and draw over all the lines using an iron-on transfer pencil. Turn the paper over again, place it on the T-shirt pencil side down and iron, following the pencil manufacturer's instructions.

2 Place a sheet of plastic or a magazine inside the T-shirt to prevent the paint from soaking through to the back. Paint the motif with black fabric paint and leave to dry.

3 Embellish the design with little spots of 3-D purple fabric paint.

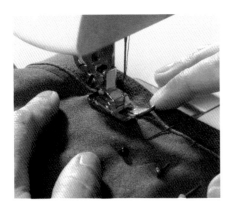

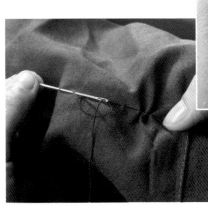

4 Right sides together, starting from one side seam and leaving the same amount of excess fabric overhanging on each side of the seam, pin one long edge of the scarf all the way around the bottom hem of the T-shirt.

5 Machine stitch the scarf to the hem. Hand stitch one line of elasticated thread down from the base of each side seam to the base of the scarf, so that the fabric gathers. If you wish, add swirls and circles of 3-D paint along the scarf, too.

Tangerine dream

This delightful little prima ballerina's tutu in hot shades of tangerine orange and poppy red, is a riot of colour and can be made in a matter of minutes – ideal when you need to create a little girl's party outfit at short notice. The design would work just as well in pastel shades. Add a magic wand and perhaps a sparkly silver crown – and hey presto! You've got a costume fit for a fairy princess!

1 Work out how long you want the skirt to be, then cut a piece of netting to twice this length and four times the width of the T-shirt. Cut a second piece of netting in a toning shade 10 cm/4 in. shorter than the first and the same width. Fold each piece of netting in half lengthways and place the shorter piece on top of the longer one, aligning the folded edges.

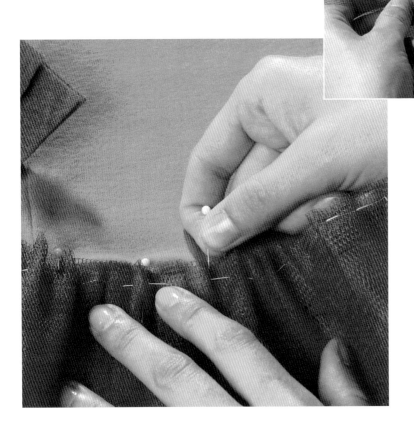

2 Tack the two pieces of netting together along the folded edges, then gently pull the tacking thread to gather the fabrics to about 3 cm/1 in. more than the circumference of the T-shirt, spacing the gathers as evenly as possible so that the skirt will hang neatly.

YOU WILL NEED

- Round-necked sleeveless T-shirt
- Tulle or netting in two toning colours
- Tape measure and ruler
- Fabric scissors
- Needle and tacking thread
- Sewing machine
- Matching sewing threads
- 12-mm-/½-in.-wide red satin ribbon
- Template on page 124
- Tracing paper and pencil
- White paper or thin card
- Scrap of felt
- Decorative button

3 Pin the gathered edges of the netting along the bottom hem of the outside of the T-shirt, and machine zigzag stitch the pieces together. Remove the tacking thread. Attach thin strips of gathered netting in a similar way around the armholes and a contrasting strip across the chest.

TIP

Keep adjusting the gathers, spacing them evenly along the length of the fabric, as you pull the thread. If necessary, adjust them again once you've pinned the netting to the T-shirt. This is probably the most time-consuming part of the whole project, but it's worth the effort in order to get the skirt to hang neatly and evenly.

4 Cut a length of 12-mm-/½-in.-wide red satin ribbon long enough to go all around the T-shirt, plus 40 cm/16 in. Fold it in half to find the centre point. Unfold, then align the centre of the ribbon with one side seam. Pin the ribbon over the netting to hide the seam, then slipstitch it in place by hand along the top and bottom edges.

A TOUCH OF SPARKLE

Using a glass or plastic button as the flower centre provides a sparkly finishing touch that little girls will simply adore, while the layers of netting and felt make convincingly three-dimensional 'petals'.

5 Copy the flower template on page 124 at 100 per cent, trace it onto white paper or thin card, and cut out. Draw around the template once on felt and twice on each colour of netting.

6 Place the netting flowers on the felt flower, alternating the colours, with the button on top. Place the whole flower on the red ribbon, near the side seam, and sew the button through all layers to attach the flower to the skirt.

Angel wings

For cool Yule clothing with a difference, adorn the back of your little cherub's plain white T-shirt with fluttering wings – and add a suitably angelic motto for a truly heavenly finishing touch! The motto is written using 3-D fabric paint, so it's slightly raised from the surface of the fabric.

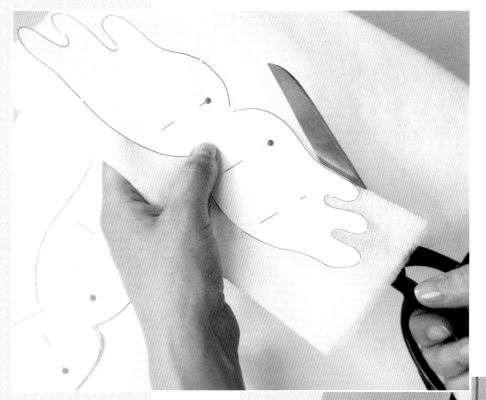

1 Copy the motif on page 125 at 100 per cent, trace it onto white paper or thin card and cut out. Fold the white cotton fabric for the wings in half, wrong sides together. Pin the template on top and cut out, cutting through both layers. Pin the template to the wadding and cut out one wing shape.

2 Cut a small piece of hook-and-loop tape. Machine stitch one piece to the centre back of the T-shirt, 10 cm/4 in. down from the neck. Stitch the corresponding piece to the middle of one of the fabric wings, on the right side of the fabric.

YOU WILL NEED

- Round-necked T-shirt
- Template on page 125
- Tracing paper and pencil
- White paper or thin card
- Scissors
- White cotton fabric
- Polyester wadding
- Hook-and-loop tape
- Sewing machine
- Lilac fabric paint
- Small paintbrush and water
- Needle
- Silver embroidery thread
- 3-D silver fabric paint

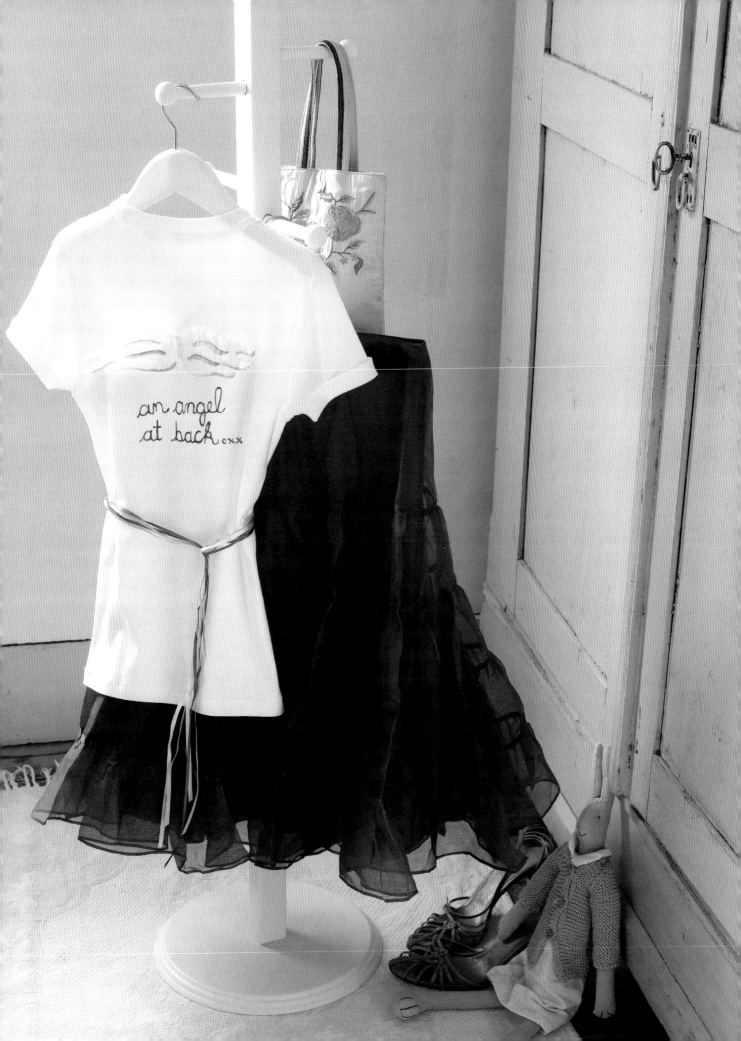

3 Dilute the lilac fabric paint with water. Paint highlights along the bottom and middle of the set of wings without the hook-and-loop tape. Fix the paint, following the manufacturer's instructions.

4 Lay the taped set of wings right side down, with the wadding on top, and the painted wings right side up on top of the wadding. Pin together. Using silver embroidery thread, work a line of running stitches all around the edges, stitching through all three layers.

5 Work more running stitches along the tops of the painted highlights, again stitching through all three layers.

6 Using 3-D paint, write your motto below the tape on the back of the T-shirt, making sure it will not be hidden when the wings are in place. Press the taped wing onto the tape on the T-shirt to secure.

A WAY WITH WORDS

If you're not confident about your ability to write the motto freehand, print it out on thin paper from your computer, using a font that looks like handwriting. Turn the paper over and draw over all the lines using a heat-transfer pen. Place the paper on the T-shirt, ink side down. Iron, following the transfer pen manufacturer's instructions, and then go over the words with the 3-D fabric paint.

MOTIF GALLERY

Use the same simple techniques to create different painted motifs to attach to the back of your T-shirt. Here are some examples that you might like to copy, but do experiment and create your own unique T-shirt motifs.

Paint the eyes and nose first, then paint the whole of the cat's face with diluted black paint. Use thicker paint to define the eyes.

Paint the features with diluted black paint, then use thicker paint to create shading. Apply grey and white paint along the bottom edge.

Paint the pirate's bandana and features first, then colour his skin with diluted pink paint.

Start by painting the grey rocket boosters and then the red rocket, leaving a space for the window. Then paint in the flames and the smoke.

Simple snowman

Appliqué simple snowmen shapes to a long-sleeved T-shirt, and add a cosy and colourful woollen collar and cuffs to keep out the winter chills – perfect attire for snowball fights and sledging! The appliqué shapes can be cut from old T-shirts that have seen better days, so this is a very economical design.

YOU WILL NEED

- Round-necked, long-sleeved T-shirt
- Woollen fabrics cut from old scarves and jumpers
- Pins
- Needle and sewing thread
- Scissors
- Templates on page 124
- Tracing paper and pencil
- Scraps of white, black and red jersey fabric
- Fabric adhesive
- 2 large buttons

1 Wash the woollen fabrics at 30 degrees higher than specified on the care label to felt the fabrics slightly and prevent them from fraying. This also means that the woollen fabrics will not shrink any further when the T-shirt is washed. Cut the fabrics into 19 x 3.5-cm/7½ x 1½-in. pieces. Reserve three pieces to decorate the cuffs and front. Pin the remaining pieces around the neck opening in several layers, to form a collar.

2 Hand stitch the pieces to the neck opening and to each other, using small stitches. Remember to make sure the child can still pass his or her head through easily!

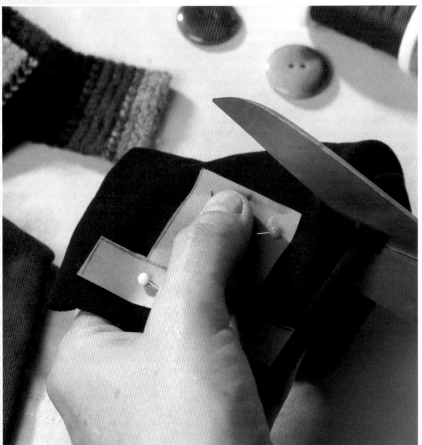

3 Enlarge the templates on page 124 by 111 per cent, trace the different elements onto white paper or thin card and cut out. Pin the snowman's body template onto white jersey fabric and cut out. Cut three more bodies, making each one 2–3 mm/⅛ in. smaller all around than the previous one. Cut two hats from black jersey fabric and two noses from red jersey fabric, making the second shapes 2–3 mm/⅛ in. smaller all around than the first.

TIPS

Stitch the appliqué pieces in place using sewing threads in colours that match the fabrics.

Don't worry if the edges of the appliqué pieces fray or curl up slightly; this adds an interesting texture and dimension to the design and the machine stitches will hold the pieces firmly in place.

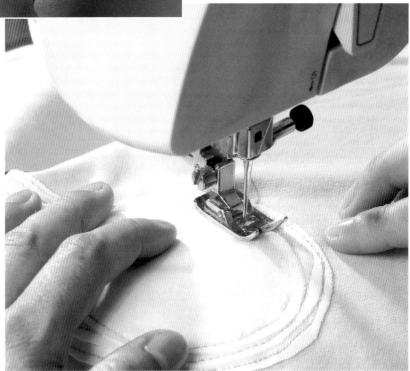

4 Glue the biggest snowman to the front of the T-shirt. When the glue has dried, machine or hand stitch around the edge using a light-coloured thread. Stitch the remaining snowmen on top, centring each motif on the previous one. Attach the hat and nose in the same way.

LAYER UPON LAYER

The appliquéd snowman is built up from several layers of fabric, each one fractionally smaller than the previous one, which gives a rounded, three-dimensional effect. Use matching thread to stitch the pieces in place.

5 Pin one of the reserved pieces of woollen fabric around each cuff and machine or hand stitch it in place. Hand stitch a large button at the point where the two ends of the woollen fabric overlap. Glue and stitch the remaining piece to the front of the T-shirt, under the snowman, at a slight angle.

Spook's skull

Indulge in a little Halloween skullduggery and transform an ordinary T-shirt into a garment that any trick-or-treater will be proud to wear. Slashes in the fabric held together with safety pins give the design an edgy, 'punk' style, while the shiny silver sequins arranged in geometric blocks have a really graphic, contemporary look. For an even spookier version, why not try painting the skull on a black T-shirt using glow-in-the-dark white or silver paint?

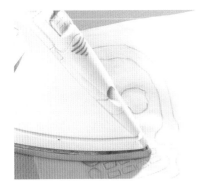

1 Copy the template on page 124 at 100 per cent, and trace it onto baking or tracing paper. Turn it over and draw over all the lines using an iron-on transfer pencil. Turn the paper over again, place it on the T-shirt and iron, following the transfer pencil manufacturer's instructions.

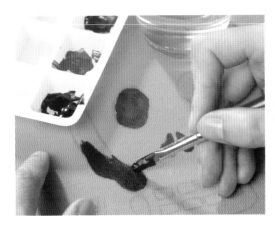

2 Put a plastic sheet or a magazine inside the T-shirt to prevent the paint from seeping through to the back. Paint the motif with black fabric paint and leave to dry.

YOU WILL NEED
- Template on page 124
- Iron-on transfer pencil
- Baking or tracing paper
- Iron
- T-shirt
- Plastic sheet or magazine
- Black fabric paint
- Paintbrush
- Iron-on silver sequins
- Small scissors
- Safety pins

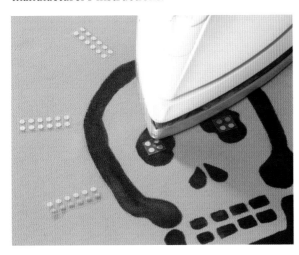

3 Following the manufacturer's instructions and referring to the photo opposite for positions, iron on small silver sequins.

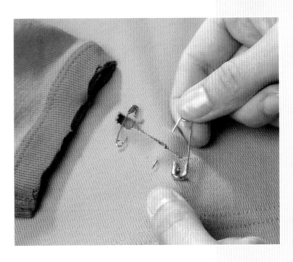

4 Cut open the cuff and neckline hems. Cut small slits on the front of the T-shirt, and pin safety pins across the slits.

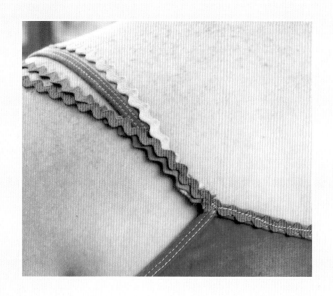

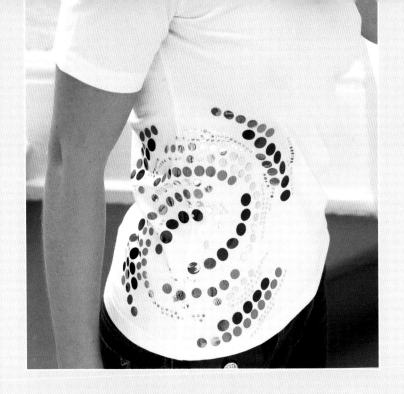

CHILLING OUT

Hand on heart

YOU WILL NEED

- Template on page 125
- Baking or tracing paper
- Fine black pen
- Iron-on transfer pencil
- Fabric scissors
- Satin bias tape
- Tacking thread
- Sewing needle
- Sewing thread to
  match bias tape
- Sewing machine
- 3-D fabric paint in
  two colours

Inspired by traditional Moroccan designs, this trimmed and painted T-shirt looks fabulous, and is easier to make than anyone will guess. Choose strong colours and sparkly paints to enhance the intricate hand motif and to reflect its exotic origins.

1 Copy the template on page 125 at 100 per cent and trace it onto baking or tracing paper. Draw over all the lines with a fine black pen.

2 Turn the baking or tracing paper over. Using an iron-on transfer pencil, carefully draw over the back of all the traced lines.

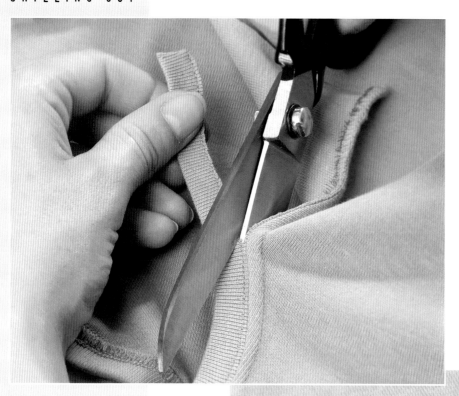

3 Using fabric scissors, cut off the T-shirt neckband. Leave the neckband seam in place to prevent the fabric from fraying, but cut as close to it as possible.

4 Tack bias tape in a contrasting colour around the neckline.

TIP

For a neat finish, mitre the bias strips at the corners of the neckline.

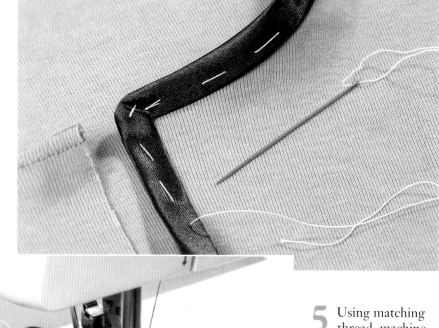

5 Using matching thread, machine stitch the bias tape in place, stitching as close to the edge of the tape as possible.

DELICATE DETAILS

To complete the design, draw tiny decorative motifs freehand around the cuff and neckband hems using 3-D fabric paint, centring them within the hemline. You can either make up the motifs yourself, or repeat an element from the main motif – but keep them very small and make sure you space them evenly.

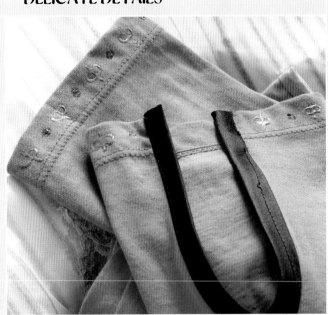

6 Place the baking or tracing paper pencil side down on the front of the T-shirt and iron, following the transfer pencil manufacturer's instructions.

7 Carefully draw over the lines of the motif with 3-D fabric paint and leave to dry.

Designer labels

Clothes manufacturers put a lot of money and effort into designing attractive labels – so why not unpick your favourites and use them to jazz up a plain T-shirt? We arranged our labels in a simple heart shape, but you could opt for a completely abstract pattern if you prefer.

YOU WILL NEED

- V-necked T-shirt
- Assorted clothes labels
- Seam unpicker
- Sewing needle
- Embroidery thread in contrasting colour
- Fabric scissors
- Fabric adhesive

1 Cut open the hems around the bottom, sleeves and neckline of the T-shirt, taking care not to cut into the stitching. Trim the opened hems in half, so that they look more like a ruffle.

2 Using a contrasting colour of thread, work a single line of running stitch around all hems, making your stitches about 0.5 cm/¼ in. long.

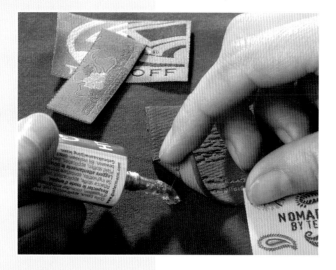

3 Using a seam unpicker, remove the labels and position them on the front of the T-shirt, overlapping them slightly to create an interesting shape.

4 When you're happy with the arrangement, glue the labels in place with fabric adhesive. Using embroidery thread in a contrasting colour, work running stitch around each label. (If the thread is too thick, use only two or three strands.)

Rickrack rock!

Tie-dyeing is a fun way of creating patterns on fabric – and if you thought it had died out with the hippy generation, think again! Here it is combined with rickrack braid in sizzlingly hot shades for a look that is thoroughly up to date and ideal for anyone who wants to revamp their wardrobe on a budget.

YOU WILL NEED

- T-shirt with thin shoulder straps
- Fabric dye
- Tacking thread
- Rickrack braid in three colours
- Fabric adhesive
- Sewing machine
- Contrasting sewing threads
- Iron-on Swarovski crystals
- Iron

1 Following the manufacturer's instructions, make up the fabric dye. Find the centre of the front of the T-shirt and fold the T-shirt along this line. Gather the fabric in your hand and tie one length of tacking thread tightly around the T-shirt for each circle, making sure you do not tie up any of what will be the back of the T-shirt. Then dye and dry the T-shirt following the dye manufacturer's instructions.

2 Glue three rows of rickrack braid around the front neckline, leaving the length of the shoulder strap plus about 2 cm/¾ in. overhanging on each side.

3 Using a contrasting colour of thread, machine stitch along the centre of each length of rickrack braid to fix it firmly in place.

TIP
The overhanging lengths of rickrack braid should be the same length as the shoulder straps. If they are too tight, they will cut into your shoulder; if they are too loose, they will slip down when you wear the T-shirt.

4 Attach one length of rickrack braid along the back neckline in the same way. Then stitch the three over-hanging lengths of rickrack braid on each side to the back neckline, securing with a small backstitch. Trim off any excess braid so that the shoulder-strap rickrack is level with the rickrack on the back neckline.

SIZZLINGLY HOT!

Rickrack shoulder straps in bright, sizzling-hot colours – lime green, deep turquoise and shocking pink – give this simple T-shirt a modern twist.

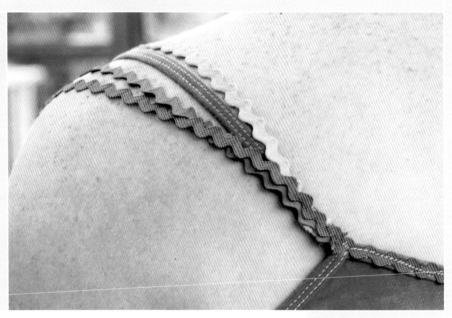

5 Following the manufacturer's instructions, iron Swarovski crystals to the centre circle on the front of the T-shirt.

Cross my heart

YOU WILL NEED

- Template on page 121
- Baking or tracing paper and pencil
- Thin paper or card
- Paper scissors
- Pins
- Scoop-necked T-shirt
- Fabric scissors
- Sweatshirt fabrics in two colours
- Fabric adhesive
- Sewing thread
- Tacking thread
- Sewing needle
- Sewing machine

For maximum impact with minimal effort, cut a heart-shaped hole in the centre of your T-shirt, and then appliqué a contrasting colour of fabric behind it. A ruffle of fabric around the neckline, in the same vibrant shade of fuchsia pink, provides a dramatic finishing touch.

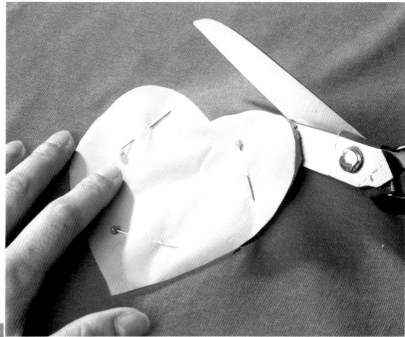

1 Copy the template on page 121 at 100 per cent, trace it onto paper or thin card, and cut out. Pin the template to the centre front of the T-shirt and carefully cut around it to make a heart-shaped hole.

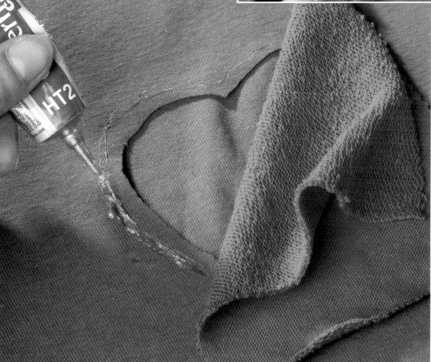

2 Cut a square of sweatshirt fabric 2.5 cm/1 in. larger all around than the cut-out heart. Turn the T-shirt inside out and apply a thin line of fabric adhesive around the edge of the cut-out heart. Place the sweatshirt fabric on top, so that the spongy side will be visible when the T-shirt is worn. Glue and then machine stitch the fabrics together.

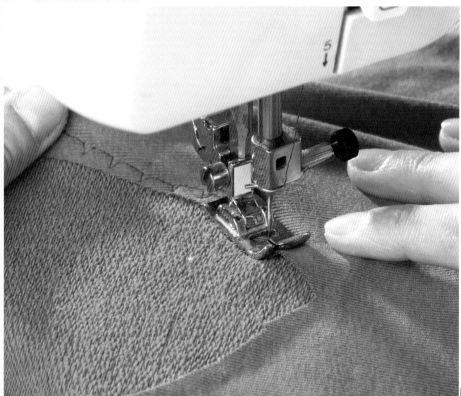

3 Machine zigzag stitch around the edge of the heart using a contrasting colour of thread.

TIP
For extra visual impact, hand stitch two or three rows of running stitch or another decorative stitch around the outline of the heart, using a contrasting colour of thread.

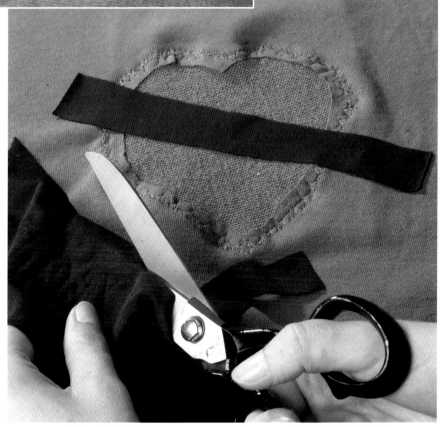

4 From the second colour of sweatshirt fabric, cut two strips about 1 cm/½ in. wide and 10 cm/4 in. longer than the heart. Tack them diagonally across the heart shape, then machine zigzag stitch them in place, using a matching colour of thread.

RUFFLED UP!

A loosely gathered strip of fabric in a contrasting colour makes a dramatic ruffled 'collar'.

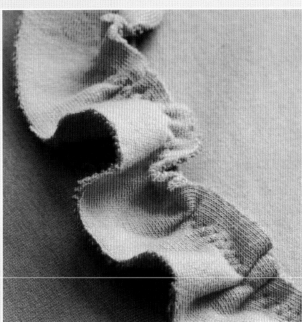

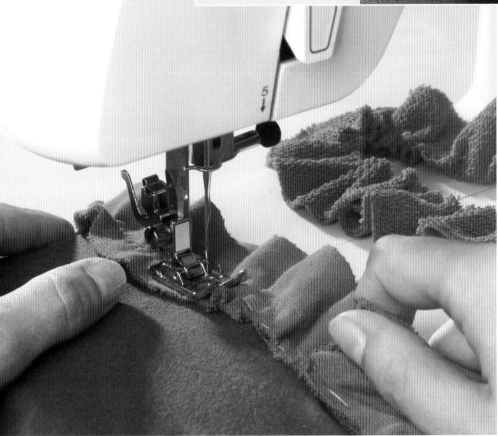

5 From the same colour of sweatshirt fabric that you used for the heart, cut bias strips 4 cm/1½ in. wide. Machine stitch them together on the short edges to make a long strip. Work a long running stitch along the length of the strip and gently pull the thread to loosely gather the fabric. Starting at one shoulder seam, pin the strip to the inside neckline about 1 cm/½ in. from the edge. Tack in place, then machine stitch with two parallel rows of stitches, one on the fabric edge and the second 0.5 cm/¼ in. below it. Remove the tacking stitches.

Denim delight

When your favourite pair of jeans gets too threadbare to wear, recycle them by cutting off the pockets and waistband and using them to embellish a denim-coloured T-shirt. Brightly coloured badges provide a trendy trim. Alternatively, use large buttons – or make your own from polymer clay.

YOU WILL NEED

- Jeans
- Denim-coloured T-shirt
- Fabric scissors
- Seam unpicker
- Pins or fabric adhesive
- Sewing machine
- Denim-coloured thread
- Colourful badges

1 Using fabric scissors, cut the back pocket off an old pair of jeans. Place it on the bottom left of the front of the T-shirt, with the base overhanging the edge. Pin or glue it in place along the side edges only. Machine stitch, using denim-coloured thread, stitching along the side edges only.

2 Cut the waistband off the jeans, cutting as close to the edge as you can.

3 Using a seam unpicker, carefully remove any belt loops from the waistband.

TIP

When you unpick the belt loops, try not to cut through any of the decorative contrast-coloured stitches along the top and bottom edges of the waistband. If you do cut through them by accident, machine stitch over the area using the same colour of thread.

4 Position the upper part of the waistband around the neck opening, with the waistband button centred on the front neck drop at its lowest point. Glue or pin it to the T-shirt. Using denim-coloured thread, machine stitch two rows of stitches 1 cm/½ in. apart all around the waistband.

ALL BUTTONED UP

The button is purely decorative, but it provides a strong focal point on the neckline of the T-shirt.

5 Pin colourful badges to the top of the pocket. If you cannot find ready-made badges that you like, you can buy a badge-making machine from most large toy stores and make your own – or use brightly coloured buttons instead.

Light as a feather

One large piece of fabric is used to make this loose-fitting, lightweight jersey T-shirt. Thin strands of embroidery thread (we used black, blue and a sparkling silver) are stitched and knotted around the neckline to provide a subtle and feathery-looking finishing touch.

1 Right sides together, fold the fabric in four, with the centrefold edges along the top and the other folded edges on the right. On the left-hand edge, mark a point 35 cm/14 in. up from the base. Draw a line down, 28 cm/11 in. in from the left-hand edge, stopping 50 cm/20 in. up from the base. Join this point with the mark on the left-hand edge.

4 Using three strands of metallic thread, insert the needle under the rolled edge, leaving 5 cm/2 in. of thread sticking out. Bring the needle back up 3 mm/⅛ in. further along. Knot the threads, then trim to 3 cm/1½ in. Repeat along the neck opening.

2 Cut along the marked lines to cut the side seams and sleeves. Starting from the right-hand (folded) edge, cut a shallow scoop about 15 cm/6 in. long along the edge of the centerfold to create the neck opening.

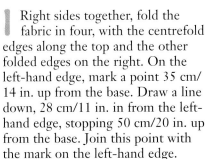

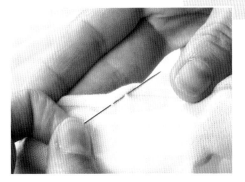

3 Unfold the shirt. Wrong sides together, machine stitch the side and armhole seams. Turn right side out. Roll the raw edges over to the outside and slipstitch, using matching thread.

5 Cut the bottom hem from one side seam to the other in a diagonal line. Measure and cut a 15-cm/6-in. vertical slit in the centre front, 12 cm/5 in. down from the neck opening. Stitch and knot three threads across the slit, about two-thirds of the way down, in the same way as along the neck opening.

YOU WILL NEED
- Jersey fabric 100 x 150 cm/40 x 60 in.
- Ruler
- Fabric marker pencil
- Pins
- Fabric scissors
- Sewing machine
- Matching thread
- Metallic embroidery thread

Sassy sashes

Drape bold, brash sashes of patterned and striped fabrics down the front of a plain T-shirt for a really casual, devil-may-care look. Use hot, clashing colours – red, pinks and purples – for a vibrant, sassy effect, or opt for greys and metallics on a black T-shirt for a look that's more punk than funk.

YOU WILL NEED
- Sleeveless red T-shirt
- Seam unpicker
- Fabric scissors
- Scraps of assorted jersey fabrics
- Pins
- Sewing machine
- Sewing thread to match the T-shirt

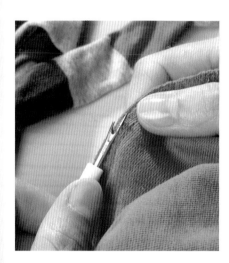

1 Using a seam ripper, open up both side seams and one shoulder seam of your chosen T-shirt and remove all loose threads.

2 Cut out strips of jersey fabrics, and knot or stitch them together. (The fabrics can be different widths.) Lay the T-shirt flat on your work surface, right side up, and place the jersey strips on top, positioning some of them diagonally across the T-shirt.

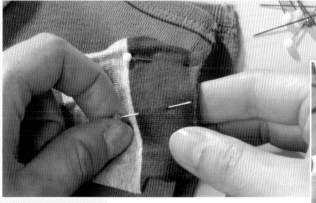

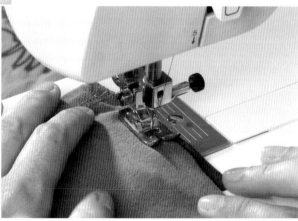

3 Once you are happy with the arrangement, pin them in place, making sure that the ends of the strips meet the side or shoulder seams. Make sure that they lay flat, and that any strips that cross the chest area are longer than the width of the T-shirt, so that the shirt will not feel too tight when it is worn.

4 Turn the T-shirt inside out and machine stitch all the seams back together, catching the jersey strips in the seams. Finally, zigzag stitch along all raw edges to prevent them from fraying.

Eastern splendour

Shisha mirrors, which are readily available from craft stores and haberdashery departments, are an inexpensive way of adding a sparkling touch of Eastern splendour to your sewing projects. Combined here with simple embroidered flowers and decorative stitching around the neckline and armholes, they transform a plain T-shirt into a garment that looks equally good with casual denim jeans or with tailored black trousers for evening wear.

1 Using fabric adhesive, glue the shisha mirrors in a V-shape around the neckline of the T-shirt. Enlarge the neck-opening template on page 121 by 180 per cent and transfer it onto the front of the T-shirt. Thread a needle with embroidery thread in a contrasting colour. Blanket stitch around the neckline (see Tips, page 66), alternating long and short stitches and keeping the stitches close together but not touching.

YOU WILL NEED
- Fabric adhesive
- Shisha mirrors
- Round-necked T-shirt
- Template on page 121
- Fabric marker pen
- Embroidery threads in colours of your choice
- Needle
- Embroidery hoop

2 To embroider the flowers, work small circles of French knots (see Tips, page 16), with another knot for the flower centre.

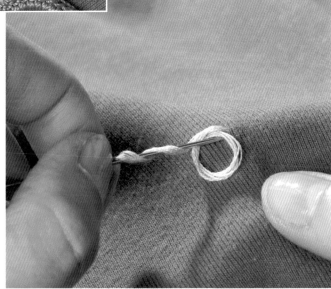

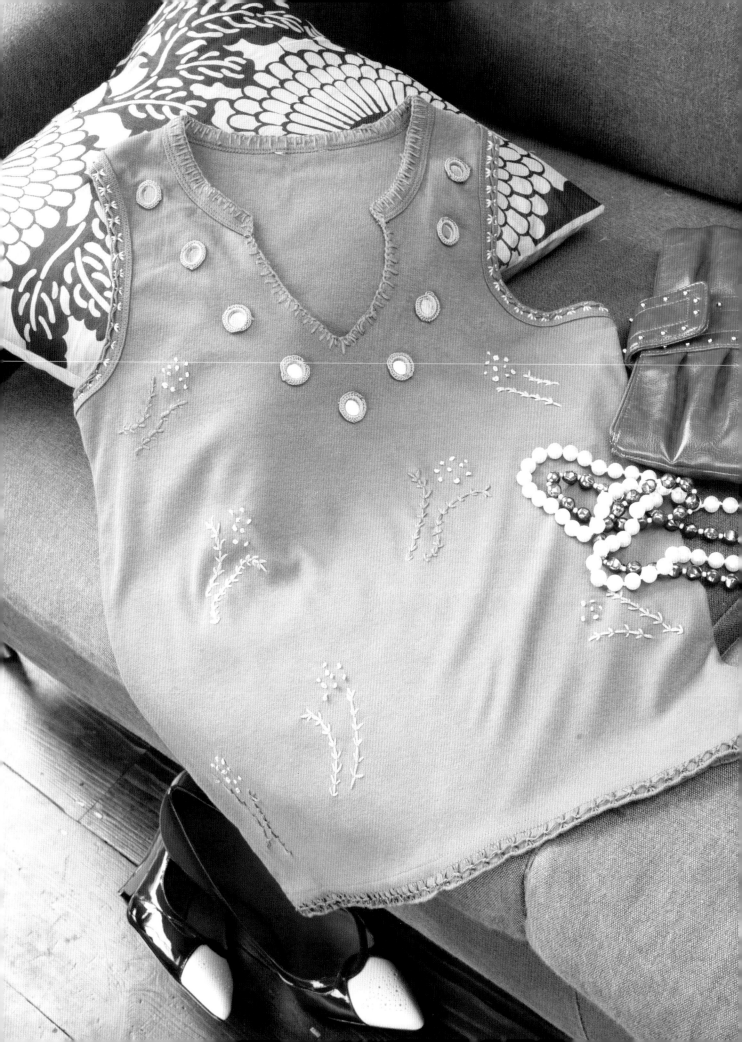

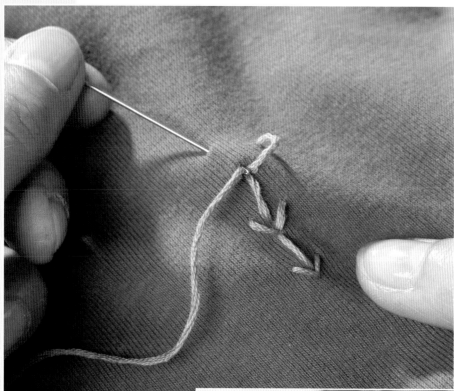

3 To make the stems, work one straight stitch along an imaginary centre line, then two diagonal stitches at 45° at the base of the straight stitch. Repeat until the stem is the length you require.

TIPS

To work the blanket stitch in Step 1, bring the needle up on the traced line of the new neckline. Take it down again on the outer line, making one straight stitch, and bring it up again on the neckline, keeping the thread around the needle tip. Pull through to secure.

When working the flower stems in Step 3, make the straight stitches longer than the diagonal stitches – anything up to twice the length.

In Step 4, space the groups of stitches around the hems as evenly as possible and try to keep them all the same length.

4 Around the bottom hem and arm-holes, work groups of three straight stitches 2–3 mm/⅛ in. apart, with a 5-mm/¼-in. gap in between each group.

SUPER STITCHING

The shisha mirrors give a wonderfully exotic sparkle to this T-shirt, while the blanket stitches accentuate the lovely, curving shape of the neckline. The embroidery around the arms, in two tones of blue, is more subtle in colouration so that it does not detract from the main embellishments.

5 Bring out a contrasting colour of thread at the start of each group of straight stitches, halfway up. Pass the needle under all three stitches, loop the thread over the needle tip and pull through. Take the needle back through to the back of the fabric at the point at which it first emerged, and pull gently to close the loop. Repeat all around the bottom and armhole hems.

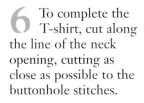

6 To complete the T-shirt, cut along the line of the neck opening, cutting as close as possible to the buttonhole stitches.

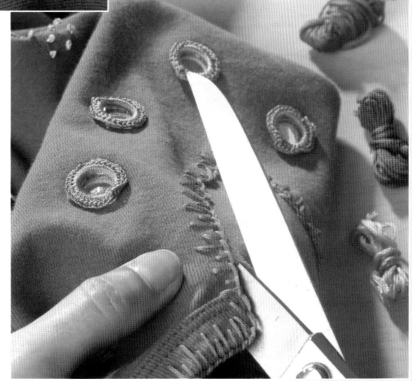

Starburst

Mix and match! Take two plain T-shirts in different colours and swap the sleeves over to create a multicoloured design. Add recycled star motifs from old T-shirts and sweatshirts and a handy 'kangaroo-style' pouch on the front and you've got a one-off garment that's as economical as it is trendy.

YOU WILL NEED

- 2 T-shirts, same size but different colours
- Seam unpicker
- Pins
- Tacking thread
- Matching sewing threads
- Sewing machine
- Tracing paper and pencil
- Contrasting fabric for pouch
- Fabric scissors
- Printed or embroidered motifs cut from T-shirt or sweatshirt fabrics
- Fabric adhesive
- Iron-on transfer pencil
- Embroidery threads
- Embroidery needle

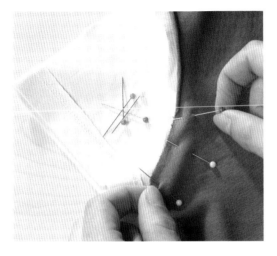

1 Unpick one sleeve on the same side of each T-shirt, swap them over and pin in place. Machine stitch, then zigzag stitch the seam allowances of both fabrics together to prevent them from unravelling.

2 Cut out the design on your fabric swatches, position them on the T-shirt and glue in place with fabric adhesive. Embroider around the edges of some of the motifs.

3 Draw the pocket shape onto a piece of fabric, and cut it out. Turn under a double hem on all sides and machine stitch. Pin in place, then machine stitch the straight sides only to the T-shirt.

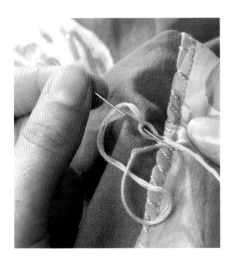

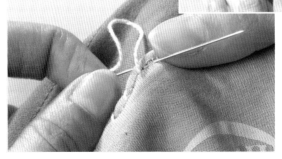

4 Hand stitch a decorative stitch around all edges, leaving the curved sides open to allow you to insert your hands into the pocket.

5 Roll the top edge of the pouch over to the outside and slipstitch using a contrasting colour of thread. If you wish, embroider a freestyle flower motif over the edge of the pouch, as we have done (see photo opposite).

Patchwork of squares

Here's a quick-and-easy way of creating a patchwork effect without having to do a lot of fiddly, time-consuming hemming and piecing. Iron the patches in place, then simply stitch over the edges in a contrasting colour of thread so that it looks as if they've been appliquéd to the T-shirt by hand.

1 Cut 8-cm/3-in. squares of fabric and the same number of squares of fusible webbing. We used nine squares, but you can use more or fewer to suit your own tastes; the fabric squares should all be roughly the same weight.

YOU WILL NEED
- T-shirt
- Fabric scissors
- Scraps of fabrics in toning shades
- Fusible webbing
- Iron
- Sewing needle
- Sewing threads

2 Following the manufacturer's instructions, iron a piece of fusible webbing to the back of each fabric square. Lay the fabric pieces on the front of the T-shirt, overlapping them slightly in places. When you're happy with the arrangement, iron them in place.

3 Thread your needle with a sewing thread in a contrasting colour. Work straight stitches over the edge of each patch. When you reach the end of each patch, bring the needle up to the front of the T-shirt, and leave the left-over thread dangling on the outside of the T-shirt.

Cool cat

For cat lovers everywhere, a charming appliqué design of a really cool feline! Lightly ruffled sleeves in toning colours add a pretty, feminine finish. The key to this project is to select small-print fabrics; if the prints are too large, they will overpower the motifs.

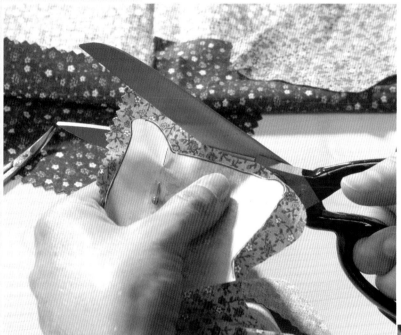

1 Enlarge the cat template on page 123 by 140 per cent, trace it onto tracing paper and cut out. Pin the template to your chosen fabric and cut out, leaving 1 cm/½ in. all around.

2 Cut small notches into the seam allowance so that, when you appliqué the motif to the T-shirt, it will lie flat and the hems will not be too bulky.

YOU WILL NEED
- Templates on page 123
- Lightweight, small-print cotton fabrics
- Pins
- Fabric scissors
- Tracing paper and pencil
- Fusible webbing
- Heat-transfer pen
- Iron
- Sleeveless T-shirt
- Sewing machine
- Matching sewing threads
- Pinking shears
- Tacking thread
- Sewing needle

3 Fold under the seam allowance and iron, so that the fabric lies really flat. Pin the cat to the T-shirt, and machine or hand stitch it in place.

TIP
Remember to reverse the lettering on a photocopier before you trace it onto the paper side of the fusible webbing – otherwise the letters will be back to front when you cut them out.

4 Following the manufacturer's instructions, apply fusible webbing to the wrong side of the fabric you have chosen for the letters and the fish. Enlarge the letters and fish templates on page 123 by 140 per cent, remembering to reverse the letters, trace them onto the webbing and cut out. Iron the bonded motifs onto the T-shirt, following the manufacturer's instructions.

SIMPLE SLEEVE

A lightly gathered strip of printed fabric in toning colours for a cap sleeve, is a really quick-and-easy way of turning a sleeveless T-shirt into something very pretty and feminine-looking.

5 Cut two strips of cotton-print fabric 4–5 cm/1½–2 in. wide and twice the circumference of the armhole in length. Cut one side of each strip with pinking shears. Work a line of tacking stitches along each strip, then gently pull the thread to gather the fabric.

6 Pin, then machine stitch the straight edge of each strip to the inside of the armhole, working one row of stitches along the edge of the armhole and a second row 5 mm/¼ in. below it.

Felted flower

Felting is an age-old technique that is currently undergoing something of a revival. In this design, bold circles of purple-toned wool are felted into the fabric itself, to create an abstract trailing pattern down one side of the T-shirt. Topped with a flamboyant felt flower brooch, the result is a stunningly original T-shirt. No two pieces of hand felting are ever exactly the same, so this really is a one-off piece that allows you to explore and develop your own creativity. The flower brooch could also be attached to a barrette-style hairgrip.

YOU WILL NEED

- Roll-necked T-shirt
- Carded wool
- Carding needle
- Sponge
- Small safety pin

1 Take filaments of carded wool and lay them out in a circular 'buckle' shape on the sponge.

2 Using the carding needle, prick the wool so that the fibres begin to felt together, leaving about 4 cm/1½ in. of the circle less heavily felted than the rest.

3 Place the partially felted circle on the T-shirt, with the less heavily felted area at the base. Place the sponge underneath. Again using the carding needle, prick through the wool and the T-shirt to attach the circle to the fabric, paying particular attention to the edges. Remove and then replace the sponge from time to time, otherwise it will end up attached to the inside of the T-shirt.

TIP

Experiment by felting wool onto scrap T-shirt fabric first to find out how far you need to felt the circles before you begin applying them to the T-shirt. If they're too heavily felted, the fibres will not be loose enough for you to push them through to the inside of the T-shirt to fix them in place. If they're too loosely felted, on the other hand, the circles will not hold their shape. Look at the photos on these pages to see the effect you should be aiming for – and remember that this is something that you will be better able to judge with practice.

4 Add more circles in the same way, overlapping the less felted areas on top of each other. (If you try to attach one well felted area to another, you will end up with a very bulky mass of fibres.)

FUNKY FELTING

The overlapping felted shapes make a lovely, flowing decoration that looks both organic and natural and very contemporary. Use wool in toning shades so that you get some variation in the colours: a single colour would look too flat and lack visual interest.

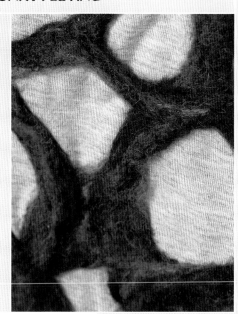

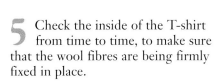

5 Check the inside of the T-shirt from time to time, to make sure that the wool fibres are being firmly fixed in place.

6 Make three circles of wool in different sizes and fill them in completely with wool fibres. Partially felt them on the sponge, in the same way as the circles, then fix them together by placing them on top of one another and pricking the centre. Partially felt a small ball of wool on the sponge, then place it in the centre of the petals and prick around the edges to attach it. Pin the flower to the T-shirt.

Studded sensation

Iron on 'metal' studs and use a simple appliqué technique to decorate a plain grey T-shirt with a brilliantly bold paisley pattern. Almost no sewing is required, so this is a really quick-and-easy project to make – start it in the afternoon and wear your new T-shirt out the same evening.

1 Using fabric scissors, care-fully cut out a selection of paisley shapes from the fabric. Cut neatly and as close to the edges of the shapes as you can.

2 Lay each paisley shape right side up on fusible webbing. Using a black pen, draw around the the shapes. Draw as close to the edge of the fabric as possible, but be careful not to mark the fabric with the pen. Using paper scissors, cut out the shapes, cutting just inside the drawn lines.

TIPS

If your paisley motifs are very small, it may be easier to use fine-pointed embroidery scissors to cut out them out.

Projects like this are a great way of making an expensive piece of printed fabric go a long way, as you need only a small number of cut-out motifs for one garment. You could use exactly the same technique for home-furnishings projects, such as pillows or table linen.

3 Following the manufacturer's instructions, iron the glue side of the fusible webbing to the back of the paisley motifs.

4 Place the shapes on the T-shirt, move them around until you're happy with the arrangement, and then iron the motifs in place. This will hold the motifs securely while you sew them in place.

COLOUR COORDINATED

At first glance, it's hard to tell that the motifs have been appliquéd to the T-shirt fabric: the T-shirt matches the pale taupe colour in the paisley motifs so well that it almost looks as if they were printed directly onto the garment.

5 Carefully slipstitch around the edge of each piece to fix the pieces securely to the T-shirt, making your stitches as small and invisible as possible.

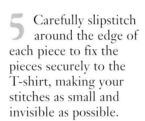

6 Following the stud manufacturer's instructions, arrange metal studs on the front of the T-shirt in abstract, curving patterns and iron them in place.

Spiralling sequins

A swirling pattern of iron-on sequins in sparkling silver and turquoise on one side seam, balanced on the other side by a sleeve gathered with a strip of bright turquoise fabric – a stylish but oh-so-simple way of stamping your own mark on a plain white T-shirt!

1 Position the sequins on the T-shirt in your chosen pattern; we arranged them in circles and spirals around the right-hand side seam. Iron them to the shirt, following the manufacturer's instructions.

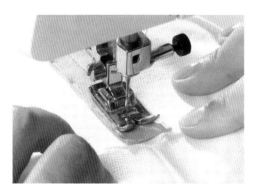

4 Machine stitch around three sides of the bias tape, leaving the sleeve end open. Then machine stitch along the tacked centre line, leaving 1 cm/½ in. unstitched at the shoulder-seam end. Remove the tacking stitches.

2 Cut a piece of bias tape the same length as the circumference of the armhole plus 1 cm/½ in. Cut one end of the tape into a V-shape and turn under the other end by 1 cm/½ in.

3 Tack the bias tape to the top of the left-hand sleeve, with the turned-under end of the tape level with the shoulder seam. Tack along the centre of the bias tape.

5 Attach one end of the ribbon or cord to a very small safety pin, then feed the pin up through one channel in the bias tape and down through the other. Pull the ribbon or cord to gather the sleeve, then tie in a bow.

YOU WILL NEED

- Short-sleeved T-shirt
- Iron-on sequins
- Iron
- 2-cm-/¾-in.-wide bias tape in contrasting colour
- Tacking thread
- Sewing needle
- Sewing machine
- Thread to match bias tape
- 3-mm/⅛-in. ribbon or cord
- Small safety pin

Belted beauty

Hark back to the 1960s and '70s with a 'chain belt' stitched from big, bold circles of luxurious silks. It looks elaborate, but is actually incredibly simple to make: all you need is a very basic sewing machine and a little patience! The belt is balanced by a single circle in the top left of the T-shirt in a contrasting colour.

1 Following the manufacturer's instructions, iron a piece of fusible webbing to the wrong side of the first piece of silk fabric.

2 On the backing paper side, draw circles 6–9 cm/ 2½–3½ in. in diameter. Cut them out.

YOU WILL NEED

- Two pieces of silk fabric
- Compass
- Fusible webbing
- Iron
- Fabric scissors
- Sewing machine
- Matching sewing threads
- T-shirt
- Necklace clasps
- Small eyelets
- Eyelet setter

3 Place the circles on the second silk fabric, wrong sides together, and iron them together, following the manufacturer's instructions.

4 Cut out the circles again; they now have a different fabric on each side. Fold them in four and cut off the tip in a curving line, leaving a border of at least 1.5 cm/¾ in. on the outside edge. When you unfold the fabric, you will have a circle with a hole in the centre.

5 Machine zigzag stitch around the inside and outside edges of each circle, matching the bobbin thread to the fabric underneath and the needle thread to the fabric on top. Sew the circles together at the edges to make a 'belt' as long as the width of the T-shirt.

TIPS

In Step 4, to ensure that the holes in the circles are completely round, place the point of a compass at the tip of the folded fabric and draw a faint pencil line around the quarter circle.

When you stitch the circles together in Step 5, arrange them in a line that slopes down towards the centre on each side rather than in a straight line, as this echoes the way in which a chain belt would naturally hang.

CHAIN REACTION

Vary the sizes of the silk circles, and alternate heavily patterned fabrics with ones that have larger areas of solid colour, so that the individual chain 'links' stand out clearly.

6 Sew a necklace clasp to each side seam at waist level. Set a small eyelet into the first and last circle of the belt, then attach the belt to the necklace clasps.

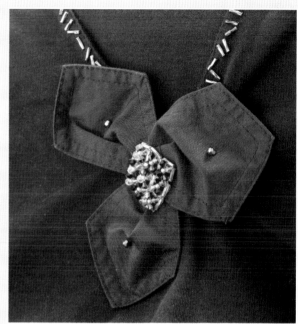

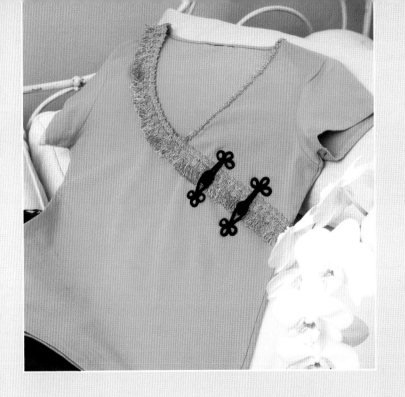

DRESSING UP

Beaded flower

A classic-shaped black top with just a hint of sparkle is always a safe bet for evening wear and can be worn by young and old alike. Here, a three-petalled flower, with a centre of black and silver beads, provides an eye-catching focal point that can be made in minutes.

1 Using a beading needle and black thread, hand stitch black bugle beads around the neckline and armholes of the T-shirt. Stitch the beads at slanting angles for a random effect.

YOU WILL NEED

- V-necked, sleeveless black T-shirt
- Black bugle beads
- Beading needle
- Black thread
- Template on page 122
- Paper or thin card
- Fabric scissors
- Black satin-effect fabric
- Sewing machine
- Fabric adhesive
- Assorted black and silver beads in different shapes and sizes
- Sewing needle

2 To make the 'petals', trace the template on page 122 onto paper or thin card, pin to black satin-effect fabric, and cut out, leaving 5 mm/¼ in. all around as a hem allowance. Cut three petals in total.

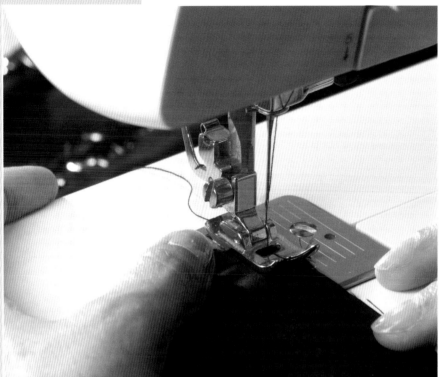

3 Machine stitch a line of stitching as decoration 1 cm/½ in. from each petal's edge all the way round.

TIPS

Mitre the corners of the petals for a neat finish.

Make sure that you completely cover the card with beads in Step 5, so that no white shows through.

4 Turn under the hem allowance on each petal, and machine stitch all around the edges, parallel to the first line of stitches to prevent the edges from fraying.

FLORAL FANTASY

The flower 'petals' are strips of black, satin-effect fabric held in place with tiny buttons or beads, while the 'centre' is a jewel-encrusted square that will catch the light and provide a glamorous sparkle.

5 Cut a piece of card about 5 cm/2 in. square and a piece of black fabric 5 mm/¼ in. larger all around. Centre the card on the wrong side of the fabric, apply fabric adhesive to the card, and fold the excess fabric over. Using tweezers, stick an assortment of jet black and silver beads to the adhesive so that the card is completely covered. Leave to dry.

6 Place the petals on the T-shirt, arranging them at an angle. Stitch a small black bead or button through each petal and the front of the T-shirt to fix them in place. Centre the bead-covered card on the petals and slipstitch around the edges.

Halter-necked triangle top

YOU WILL NEED

- Scarf 1 m/3 ft square
- Fabric scissors
- Pins
- Sewing machine
- Matching thread
- Sewing needle
- Silver ring 5 cm/ 2 in. in diameter
- 1.8 m/2 yds length of 1-cm-/½-in.-wide satin ribbon
- Zipper

For a stylish outdoor party on a balmy summer's evening, turn a large scarf into an elegant halter-necked top. A silver ring at the neckline makes a striking focal point, and satin-ribbon ties add a hint of opulence. You can make two tops from one scarf, so this project is great value for money.

1 Fold the scarf in half diagonally from corner to corner, then cut along the fold to obtain two triangles.

2 Turn under and pin a double hem along the two short sides of one triangle, and machine stitch, using matching thread.

3 Loop the top corner of the triangle through the ring. Slipstitch along the folded-over side edges to hold the ring in place. Fold the ribbon in half, loop it through the ring, and pull taut.

4 Wrap the triangle around your body to work out how much you have to take in for the back seam. Cut off the excess fabric, leaving enough to turn under a double hem on each side. Turn under the hems, pin a zipper of the correct length in place, and machine stitch to secure.

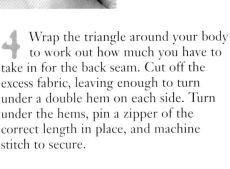

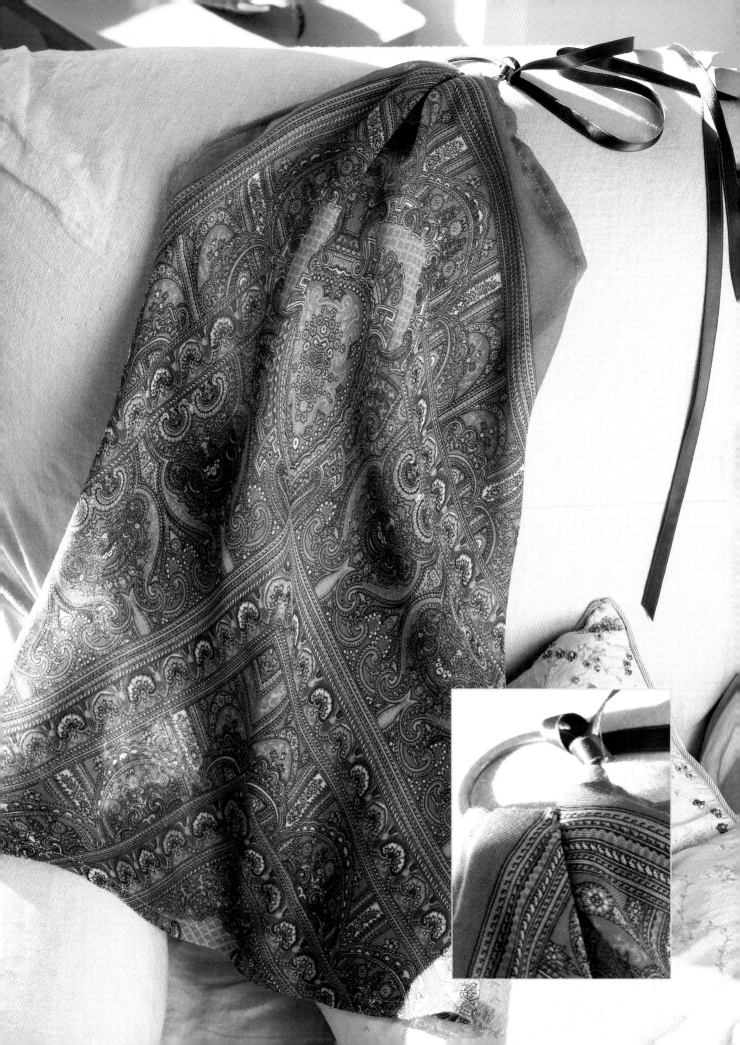

Two-tier top

For that trendy layered look, take two T-shirts in toning shades and stitch one on top of the other. What could be simpler? Add a bunch of sparkling sequin ribbons at the neckline and you've got a colorful top in which you can dance the night away – and all for just a few minutes' work!

YOU WILL NEED

- 2 sleeveless T-shirts in toning shades, one 1 size larger than the other
- Fabric marker pencil
- Ruler
- Fabric scissors
- Needle
- Matching sewing thread
- Sequin ribbon
- Safety pin

1 Cut off the bottom hems of both T-shirts, making sure you do not cut through the stitching. Cut the cut-off sections of hem into ribbons about 12 cm/5 in. long.

2 On the larger shirt, draw a line down the centre front, from the neck opening to the bottom, using a light-coloured fabric marker pencil.

3 Using fabric scissors, carefully cut along the marked line, stopping 5 cm/ 2 in. below the neckline.

4 Place the larger T-shirt over the smaller one. Using matching sewing thread, hand stitch the T-shirts together along the shoulder seamline.

TIP

Pin the T-shirts together along the shoulder seam, so that they cannot slip out of position while you are stitching.

5 Tie the cut ribbons around the closed side of the safety pin. For a touch of glamour, add some sequin ribbons, too. Pin the safety pin across the top of the centre slit in the larger T-shirt, so that it looks as if it's holding the T-shirt closed.

Flower power

Combine freestyle machine embroidery with funky, black-leather flower shapes for a trendy, contemporary take on the age-old technique of appliqué. Choose a T-shirt in a strong, modern colour rather than a neutral, earthy shade: we used a rich, turquoise blue, but fuchsia pink or a zingy orange would work just as well.

1 Trace the templates on page 121 onto paper or thin card and cut out. Place the templates on the reverse side of a piece of black leather, draw around them with a white marker pencil, and cut out. You will need four small flowers and one large one.

YOU WILL NEED

- Templates on page 121
- Tracing paper and pencil
- Paper or thin card
- Piece of black leather
- White marker pencil
- Fabric scissors
- Sewing machine
- White and black thread

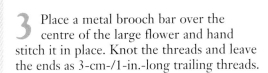

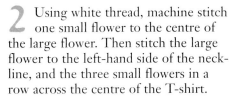

2 Using white thread, machine stitch one small flower to the centre of the large flower. Then stitch the large flower to the left-hand side of the neck-line, and the three small flowers in a row across the centre of the T-shirt.

3 Place a metal brooch bar over the centre of the large flower and hand stitch it in place. Knot the threads and leave the ends as 3-cm-/1-in.-long trailing threads.

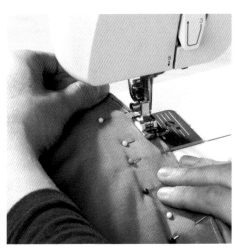

4 Embroider the leaves by machine, using white and black thread. A rough outline shape, with a central vein and one or two spurs coming off the vein, is all that is required.

5 Fold the T-shirt so that you form a line running down from each flower head, just touching the ends of the leaves. Machine stitch along the line about 5 mm/¼ in. from the fold, using white thread. This creates a narrow, raised channel for the stalk.

Poppy-red cascade

For a quick-and-easy way of jazzing up a V-necked T-shirt for a summer evening, simply attach a cascade of poppy-red and pink fabric 'flowers'. To balance the design, bunch several flowers together near the shoulder seam, and space them further apart as you move down the T-shirt.

YOU WILL NEED

- V-necked T-shirt
- Lightweight fabric in tones of red and pink
- Fabric scissors
- Compass
- Fabric marker pencil
- Needle
- Matching thread

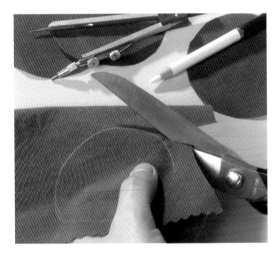

1 Using a fabric marker pencil and a compass, draw about 20 circles between 7 and 10 cm/3 and 4 in. in diameter onto different tones of red fabric. (If you haven't got a compass, draw around glasses of the appropriate size.) Cut out.

2 Fold each circle in half. Find the center of the folded edge and, using matching sewing thread, backstitch a dart 1–3 mm/$\frac{1}{16}$–$\frac{1}{8}$ in. wide from this point to the outer edge of the circle.

3 Open out the 'flowers'. Place them on the T-shirt and stitch in place. We arranged them on the left-hand side of the T-shirt, running downward from the neck seam.

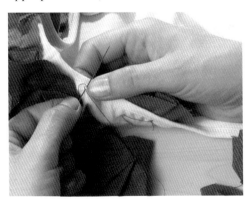

4 Attach several flowers to a thin, matching thread, leaving 3–4 cm/ 1–1½ in. between them. Attach the thread to the shoulder seam, allowing the flowers to hang freely down the back.

5 All our fabric flowers have raw edges. If you're worried about the fabric fraying, you can backstitch all around the edge, using either a matching or a contrasting colour of thread.

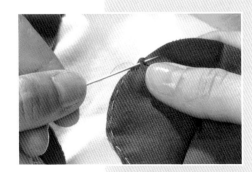

Oriental jade

You may not have thought of using home-furnishing trims such as braids or piping on clothing, but with so many wonderful colours and styles available, it's crazy not to take advantage of them! Here, we've attached two widths of braid to a jade-green T-shirt and added an Oriental-style fastening for authenticity.

1 Place the narrow upholstery trim on the left-hand side of the neck-line, running from the shoulder seam to the bottom of the V. Turn under about 5 mm/¼ in. at each end and glue in place.

YOU WILL NEED
- V-necked T-shirt
- Upholstery trims
  1 cm/½ in. and 4 cm/
  1½ in. wide
- Fabric adhesive
- Fabric scissors
- Sewing thread
- Matching ribbon
- 2 'frog' fastenings

2 Place the wider upholstery trim on the right-hand side of the neckline, running diagonally from the shoulder seam to the side seam, and glue in place, again with a turn-under at each end.

3 Using matching thread, slipstitch all around the edge of the upholstery trims to attach them firmly to the T-shirt.

TIP

The key to this design lies in keeping the colour scheme very simple, so choose decorative trims in a similar tone to the T-shirt. The stark, black fastenings provide all the colour contrast necessary.

4 Position the 'frog' fastenings on the T-shirt, spacing them evenly across the upholstery trim between the base of the V-neck and the side seam, then glue them in place.

LOOP THE LOOP

The fastenings are purely decorative rather than functional, but they are a major factor in creating the Oriental style of the design. Note how the shape of the fastenings is echoed in the curved loops of the braid.

5 Using matching sewing thread, stitch over the loops of the frogs to attach them firmly to the T-shirt. If you wish, you can also stitch the loops of the frogs over the knots so that they are permanently closed.

Collar and tie

For evening attire with a difference, take your inspiration from men's formal wear and opt for a collar and tie! Here, the collar and tie are combined in one – black sequin ribbon on one side, which will sparkle in the light, and a vibrant, Art Deco-style fabric on the other to provide a blast of colour.

YOU WILL NEED
- V-necked black T-shirt
- Fabric scissors
- Art Deco-style fabric
- Black sequin ribbon
- Matching threads
- Sewing needle
- Sewing machine
- Pen
- Ruler

1 Cut the sleeves diagonally from the side seam under the armhole to the end of the sleeve.

2 Cut the sequin ribbon as long as the neck opening of the shirt plus 60 cm/ 24 in. Cut a piece of patterned fabric 2 cm/ ¾ in. wider and 2 cm/ ¾ in. longer than the sequin ribbon. (If necessary, sew several pieces of fabric together to create one that is the right length.)

TIPS

It's important that the fabric 'tie' is exactly the same width all the way along and that the edges are sharp and neat. When you fold under the Art Deco-style fabric in Steps 4 and 5, measure it carefully. Use fabric adhesive to hold the fabrics together temporarily in Step 4, so that nothing can slip out of place while you are stitching.

3 Right sides together, centre the sequin ribbon on the patterned fabric and pin in place. Fold the corners of one edge of the patterned fabric over to the wrong side at a 45° angle to form a neat mitre and pin in place.

4 Fold under 1 cm/½ in. along one long edge of the patterned fabric, then glue and machine stitch along this edge.

5 Turn right side out, turn under the other edge of the patterned fabric, pin the ribbon, and machine stitch both pieces together.

DECO-STYLE DRAMA

The Art Deco-style patterned fabric is the perfect way to offset the blacks of the T-shirt and the sequin ribbon.

6 Position the centre of the collar on the center back neckline, with the sequin ribbon on the outside. Hand stitch the edge of the ribbon collar to the edge of neck opening, stopping 5 cm/2 in. before the base of the V-neck on each side.

7 Knot with the two end pieces of the ribbon collar; if you wish, you can sew the knot to fix it permanently.

111

Sea-blue surprise

A big, bold piece of jewellery can transform an everyday outfit into something really spectacular. Here we've sewn wooden beads in soft hues of deep blue and aquamarine around the collar of a plain grey T-shirt to create a 'necklace' that just cries out to be noticed!

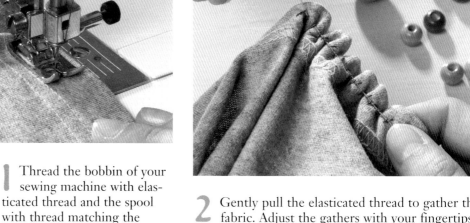

YOU WILL NEED

- Short-sleeved round-necked T-shirt 2 sizes bigger than your regular size
- Sewing machine
- Elasticated thread
- Sewing threads to match T-shirt and beads
- Lightweight blue and aquamarine wooden beads 0.5–2 cm/¼–¾ in. in diameter
- Long sewing needle

1 Thread the bobbin of your sewing machine with elasticated thread and the spool with thread matching the T-shirt. Machine zigzag one line of stitching around the cuff edges and bottom hem of the T-shirt. (Test the thread tension first on spare jersey fabric.)

2 Gently pull the elasticated thread to gather the fabric. Adjust the gathers with your fingertips until they are positioned evenly all around the cuffs and bottom hem. Knot the elasticated threads on the inside of the garment to secure.

3 Sew the beads all around the front neck opening, positioning the larger beads closer to the neck edge. If the sewing thread is too thin, double it.

4 Keep the thread taut, but not so tight that it puckers the T-shirt. Secure the beads with a double stitch on the inside of the T-shirt.

Sequinned sensation

When it comes to scoring high in the fashion stakes, grey and metallic silvers are the new black – versatile enough to work with almost anything, stylish enough to make you stand out from the crowd! In this design, silver sequin ribbon and little metallic buttons are an inexpensive way of creating that all-important sparkle that every party girl needs. Best of all, you can decorate this T-shirt in minutes, which means you've plenty of time to relax and pamper yourself before the party begins.

1 Using fabric scissors, cut off the neckband and the cuffs, cutting as close to the stitching line as possible; the remaining fabric will tend to curl around. Machine zigzag stitch down the centre front of the T-shirt, from top to bottom.

YOU WILL NEED

- Sequin ribbon of any colour and width
- Matching thread
- Fabric scissors
- Small metal buttons
- Fabric adhesive
- Sewing needle
- Sewing machine

2 Gently pull the beginning and end of the zigzag stitches to gather the fabric.

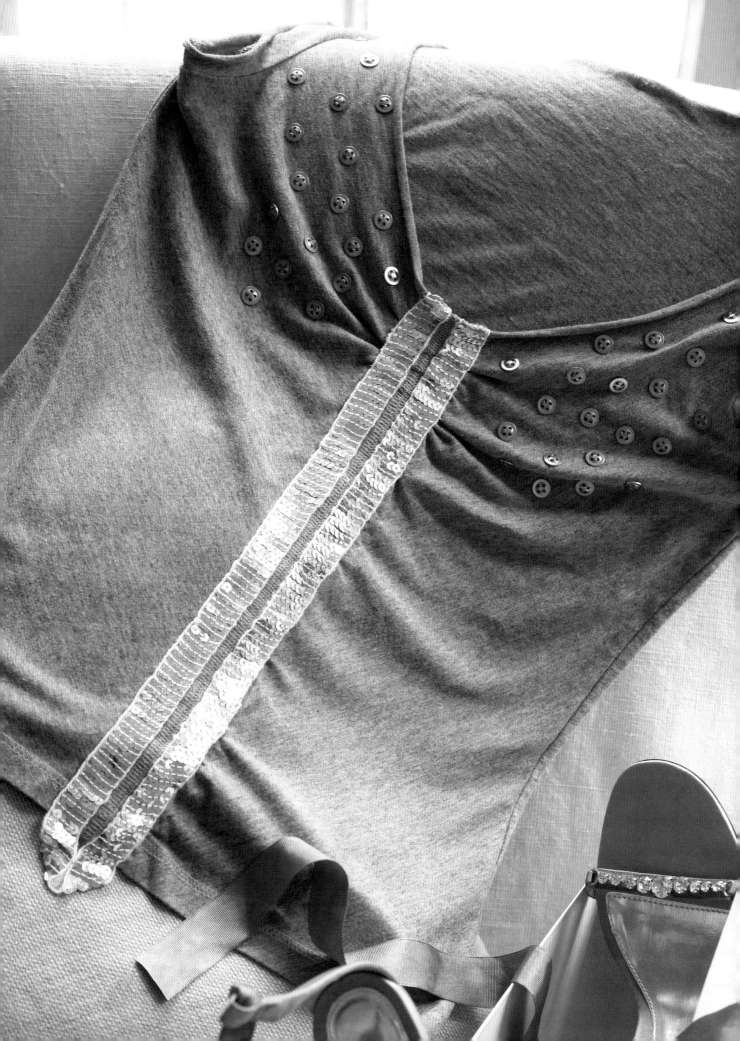

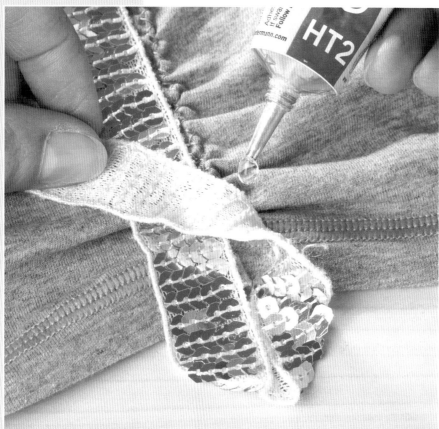

3 Position silver sequin ribbon along one side of the zigzag stitches, running from just above the neckline to the base of the T-shirt, and fix it with small dabs of fabric adhesive at regular intervals. At the base, fold the ribbon under at an angle of 45°, and then back up at 90°. Take the ribbon to the neckline on the other side of the zigzag stitches. Turn over about 5 mm/¼ in. of ribbon to the inside of the neck on each side of the line of zigzag stitches.

TIPS

Stitch as close to the edges of the ribbon as you can, so that the stitches don't go over the sequins.

When you reach the V-shaped section of ribbon at the bottom, stitch along the inner edge of one ribbon, then turn the piece around, keeping the needle in the fabric, and work your way up the other side.

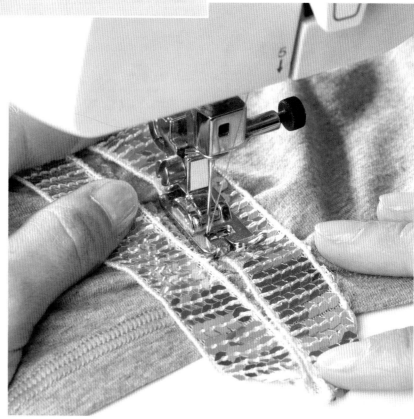

4 Using matching thread, machine or hand stitch along both edges of the ribbon to attach it firmly to the T-shirt, making sure that the zigzag stitches can still be seen in between the two rows of ribbon.

SILVERY SPARKLE

The metallic buttons and silver sequin ribbon have a matt finish, so they provide an attractive gleam without being overpoweringly bright.

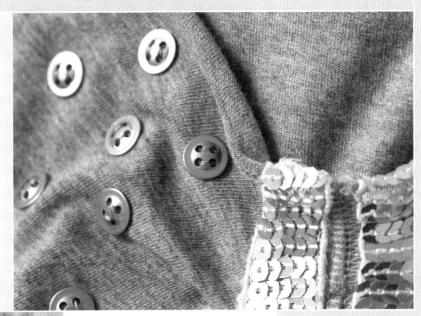

5 Place a strip of sequin ribbon along each shoulder, extending to about 8 cm/3 in. beyond the cuff, and hand stitch it in place along the shoulder seam only. Turn the excess ribbon to the inside of the sleeve, and stitch the short end to the inside, level with the armhole seam.

6 Sew small metal buttons to the front of the shirt around the neckline, positioning them randomly.

Luxurious lace

Who would guess that a humble T-shirt forms the basis of this elegant top? The tiers of delicate, ivory-coloured lace cascading down the front are a simple way of creating a sophisticated and luxurious look for a special occasion. A satin trim around the neckline provides a neat and professional finish.

YOU WILL NEED

- Round dish
- Fabric marker pen
- T-shirt
- Lace ribbon 8 cm/3 in. wide
- Fabric scissors
- Pins
- Satin bias tape
- Basting (tacking) thread
- Sewing needle
- Sewing machine
- Matching thread

1 Place a dish partially overlapping the front neck opening of the T-shirt, draw around it with a fabric marker, and cut out the new neckline with fabric scissors.

2 Cut the lace into 15-cm/6-in. lengths. Make a fold in the centre of the first piece and place it on the bottom edge of the T-shirt. Pin it down, turning under the edges. Machine stitch the top edge to the T-shirt. Repeat, fixing each piece 5–8 cm/2–3 in. above the previous one, until you reach the neckline.

4 When you come to your starting point on the centre of the back neck edge, fold the end of the bias tape to the inside before fixing it 1 cm/ ½ in. over the starting point of the bias in order to have neat start and end points (see Moroccan shirt). Using matching thread, machine stitch all around the bias tape to fix it in place.

3 Pin the last piece of lace to the centre of the front neck edge. Starting in the centre of the back neck edge, baste (tack) bias tape all around the neck opening, making sure it covers the top edge of the last piece of lace.

Templates

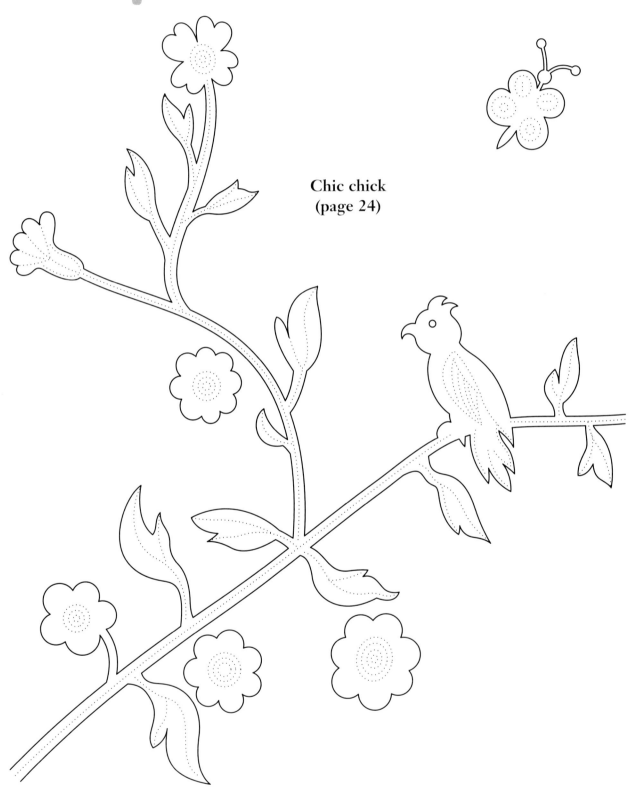

Chic chick
(page 24)

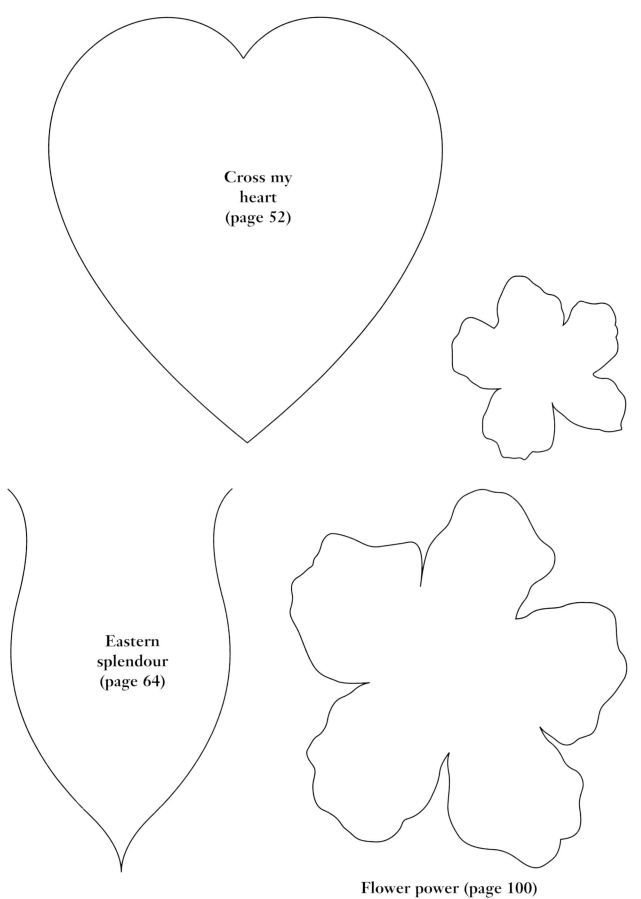

Cross my
heart
(page 52)

Eastern
splendour
(page 64)

Flower power (page 100)

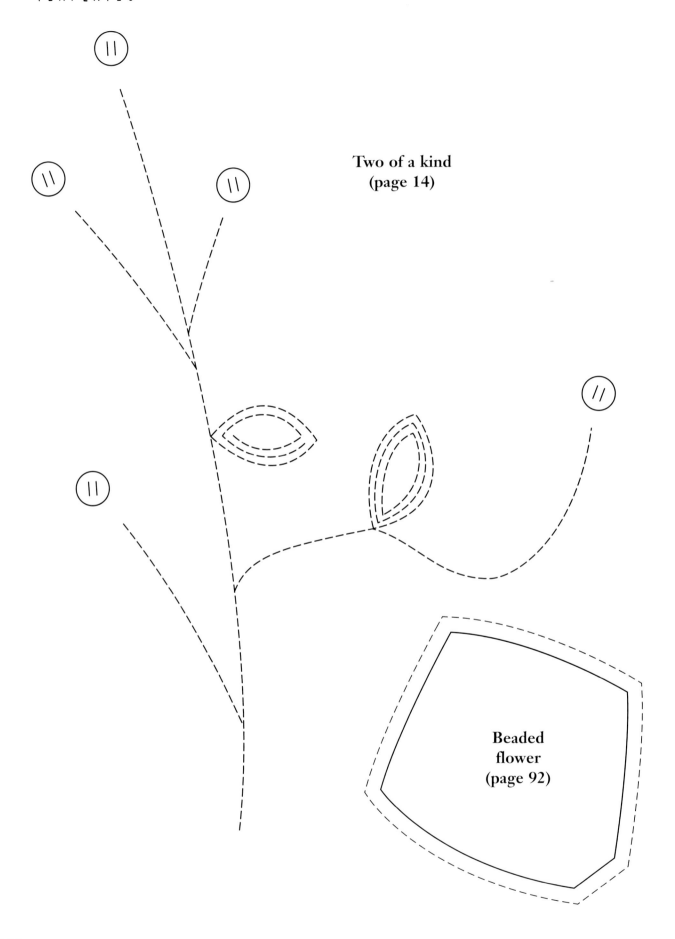

Two of a kind
(page 14)

Beaded
flower
(page 92)

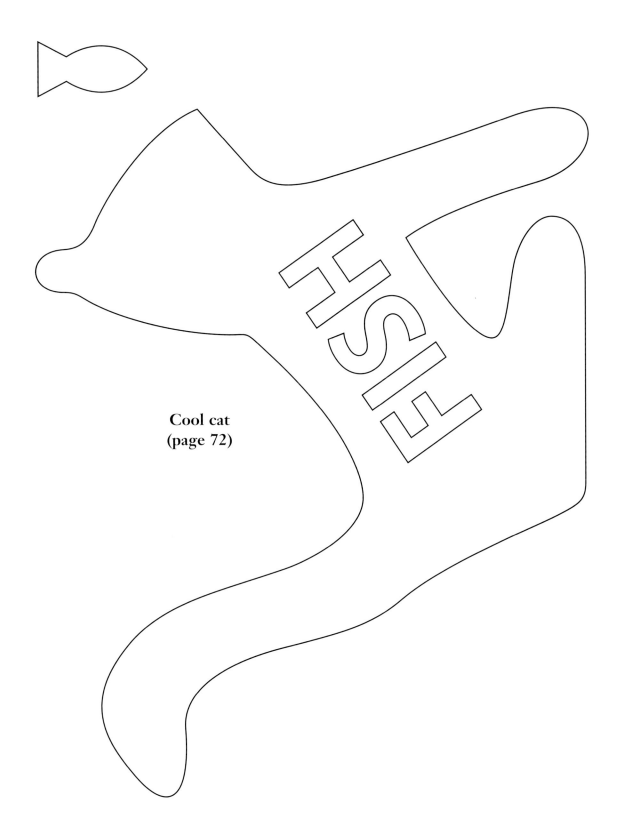

Cool cat
(page 72)

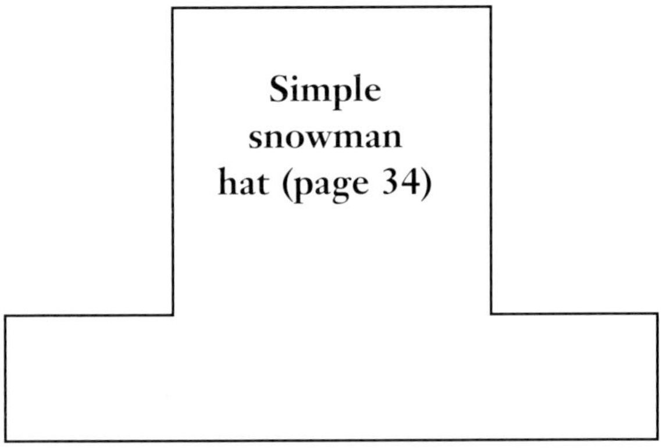

Simple snowman hat (page 34)

Tangerine dream (page 26)

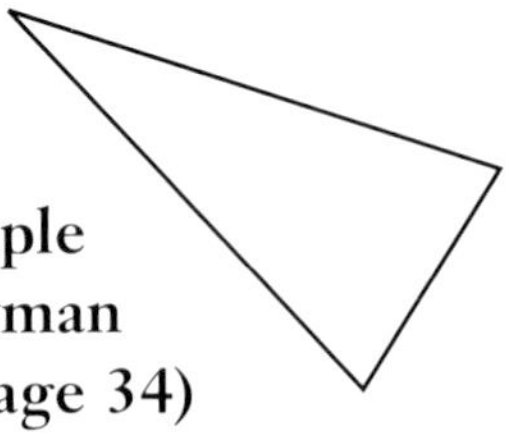

Simple snowman nose (page 34)

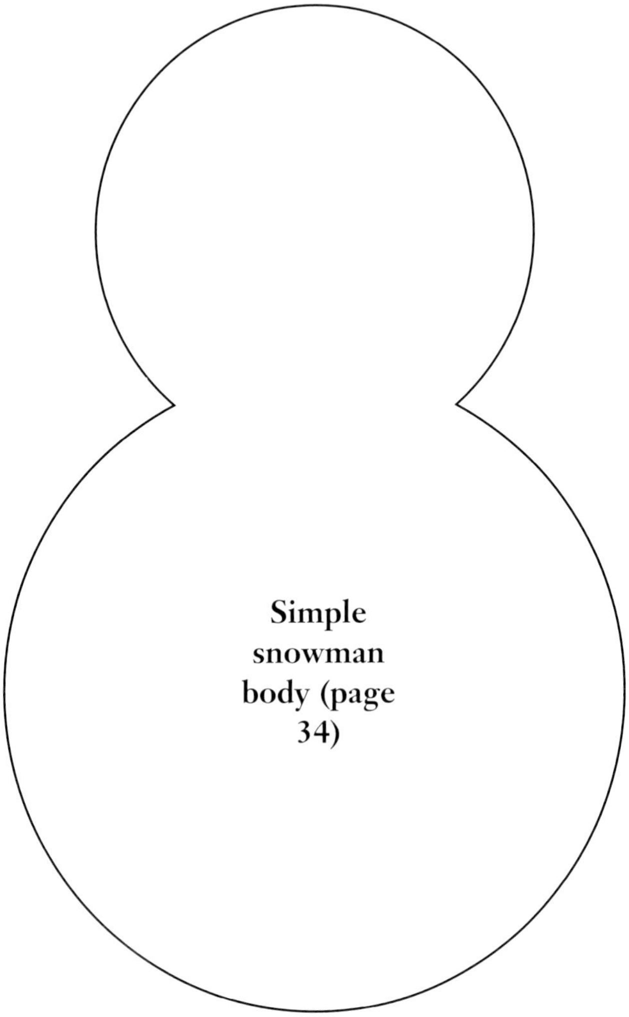

Spook's skull (page 38)

Simple snowman body (page 34)

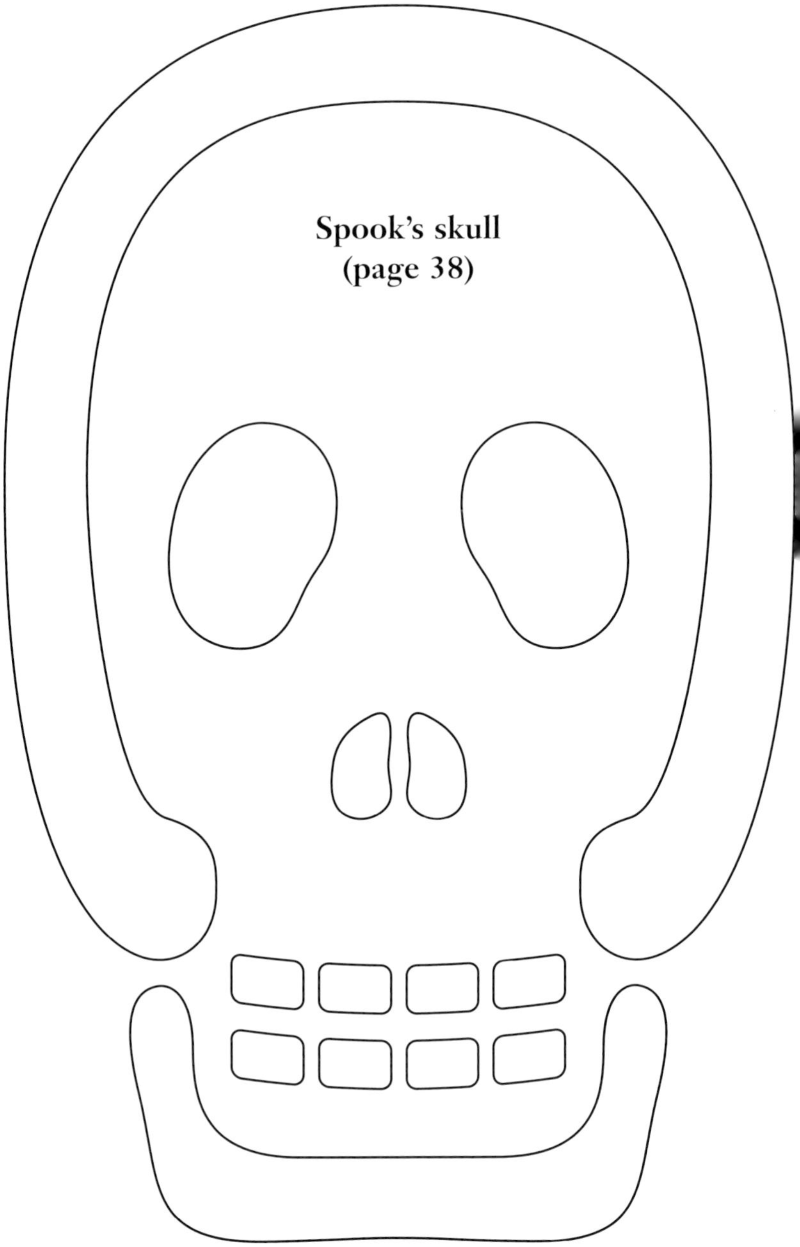

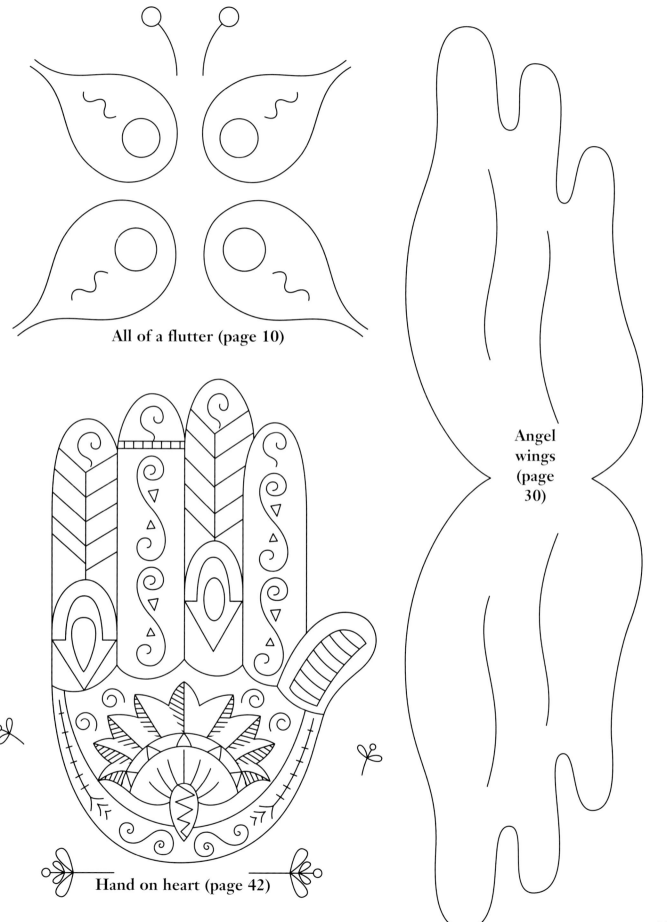

All of a flutter (page 10)

Angel wings (page 30)

Hand on heart (page 42)

Index

Also available from CICO Books

Bead & Button, Ribbon & Felt Jewellery:
35 sewing-box treasures to make & give
Deborah Schneebeli-Morrell
£12.99

Wire & Bead Celtic Jewellery:
35 quick & stylish projects
Linda Jones
£12.99

201 Crochet Motifs, Blocks, Projects and Ideas
Melody Griffiths
£14.99

Crochet in No Time:
50 modern scarves, wraps, tops and more to make
on the move
Melody Griffiths
£14.99

Felt Style:
35 fashionable accessories to create and wear
Chrissie Day
£12.99